SO-BZZ-169

CONTENTS

TRANSLATORS' PREFACE

The translation of Martin Noth's <u>Überlieferungsgeschicht-liche Studien</u>, pp. 1-110, here presented is based on a translation prepared by Jane Doull and revised by John Barton. Michael D. Rutter thoroughly reworked the translation and D.R. Ap-Thomas completely reviewed it making many corrections and improvements. David J.A. Clines supervised and edited the various transformations through which the translation passed.

An effort has been made in the present work to provide, as far as possible, a readable translation rather than an excessively literal one. Regularly recurring technical terms, however, are rendered with a degree of uniformity necessitated by the subject matter.

The system of reference to scholarly literature has been altered in order to facilitate the reader's location of the specific works referred to, and a full bibliography of works cited has been prepared. Both the endnotes and bibliography mention English translations where appropriate. The index is based on Noth's index, and incorporates a number of corrections of that index.

In citing Biblical references, Noth used the customary system of designating sub-sections of verses by letters of the Greek alphabet. These Greek letters have here been represented by elevated letters in Roman script, ^{a} standing for alpha, ^{b} for beta, and ^{c} for gamma.

FOREWORD

Martin Noth's Überlieferungsgeschichtliche Studien was first published in 1943 /1/ and consists of two main independent studies, the first dealing with the "Deuteronomistic History" comprising the corpus of literature in the Hebrew Bible from Deuteronomy to the end of 2 Kings, the second with the work of the Chronicler (1 and 2 Chronicles, Ezra, Nehemiah), and an appendix dealing with the Priestly document and the redaction of the Pentateuch. The influence of these studies upon subsequent research can scarcely be overstated and there has long been a need for a translation which would make them more widely accessible to students in English-speaking countries. The present volume begins to meet this need by providing a translation of the first of these studies, that concerning the "Deuteronomistic History", which is also the best known of them.

A very brief sketch of earlier critical investigation of this corpus will suffice to indicate the antecedents as well as the nature and significance of Noth's own study of it. At an early stage in the history of modern Pentateuchal study scholars recognised that the main sources of the Pentateuch (J,E,D,P) go beyond this literature into the book of Joshua so that one can speak of a Hexateuch. It was also recognised that the hand of a Deuteronomic editor (or editors) can be discerned in the ensuing books as well, that is, Judges, Samuel and Kings. In the late nineteenth century the view began to find favour that J and E continue beyond Joshua, and C.H. Cornill and K. Budde, for example, argued that these sources can be discerned as far as 1 Kings 2 /2/. Subsequently, especially in the 1920's, such a view gained wider support. For example, in 1921 I. Benzinger argued that J continues as far as 2 Kings 17 and E as far as the account of Josiah's reign in 2 Kings 22-23 /3/. Similarly, O. Eissfeldt argued that J and E as well as his proposed Pentateuchal source L can be traced in the Former Prophets /4/. Best known from this period is G. Hölscher's detailed contribution in 1923 in which he argued that J can be traced to the division of the kingdom in 1 Kings 12, while E continues to the end of 2 Kings /5/. Thus many scholars came to favour the same type of documentary analysis for Judges - 2 Kings as had been established in the case of the Hexateuch. The older view, according to which Judges, Samuel and Kings originated as independent books which were subsequently edited by Deuteronomic redactors was thus abandoned, though we may note here that it was later revived and argued by, for example, G. Fohrer /6/.

Opposition to a "documentary theory" of the composition of Judges, Samuel and Kings, that is, to the view that these books were composed in the same sort of way as the Hexateuch itself, was expressed in the 1920's by such scholars as R. Kittel and L. Rost. Kittel, for example, argued that these books were composed of numerous originally independent smaller literary units and complexes, though he was willing to concede that some of these may be related to the Hexateuchal sources J and E /7/. Rost, however, argued that neither J or E is to be found in these books (that P does not go beyond Joshua had been and remains agreed), and pointed, in his well known monograph of 1926 /8/, to the so-called "Succession Narrative" in 2 Samuel 9-20 + 1 Kings 1-2 as an example of the sort of originally independent source, unrelated to any of the documents of the Hexateuch, which the author of Samuel had employed. Another example is the "ark narrative" in 1 Samuel 4-6 + 2 Samuel 6.

It was the type of approach advanced by scholars such as Kittel and Rost which Noth took up and argued in detail in the study contained in the present volume. Noth now denied that any of the Pentateuchal sources J,E,P goes beyond the end of Deuteronomy, a view which he had largely moved towards in his commentary on Joshua in 1938 /9/. Instead, Noth advanced his theory that the corpus Deuteronomy - 2 Kings is the work of an author who wrote during the exilic period, though allowance is made for some further additions, some of them substantial, to this author's original work. This author had at his disposal numerous independent literary units and complexes, including the original book of Deuteronomy itself which he edited to form the first chapter, so to speak, of his history work. All this material he set out and wove together with his own insertions and comments here and there throughout it.

To describe Noth's study of Deuteronomy - 2 Kings as one of the "classics" of Old Testament research might give an incorrect impression. Often when we refer to a work as a "classic" we mean that it was such in its own time but that further developments have left its conclusions behind. Such might be our view of, for example, another of Noth's famous contributions, his monograph on the nature of pre-monarchic Israel as a twelve-tribe "amphictyony" which was published in 1930 /10/ but the main conclusions of which no longer command the widespread support they once enjoyed. This is not the case with his study of Deuteronomy - 2 Kings and herein lies the main justification for a translation of it even so long after its first publication. This is a "classic" work in the sense that it still remains the fundamental study of the corpus of literature with which it is concerned, and still provides, as far as the majority of scholars are concerned, the basis and framework for further investigation of the composition and nature of this corpus.

The view that the Former Prophets represent for the most part a continuation of the Pentateuchal sources has continued to have its advocates /11/, while, as noted above, Fohrer, for example, has favoured a different solution, though he adheres to the view that the Pentateuchal sources continue in Joshua and as far as Judges 1:1-2:5. But most scholars have accepted Noth's understanding of the composition of Deuteronomy - 2 Kings, and further developments have consisted of refinements of his analysis. Important refinements and modifications have been suggested by, for example, R. Smend, W. Richter and W. Dietrich /12/. Division of opinion remains concerning the date of the composition of the "Deuteronomistic History". Noth assigned it to the exilic period, but some, for example F.M. Cross /13/, still favour the view that a pre-exilic edition can be discerned behind the corpus in its final form. In all of this, however, Noth's study remains the fundamental work. The translation of it now provided in this volume is to be warmly welcomed.

Oriel College, Oxford   E.W. Nicholson
February 1981

NOTES

1   Halle 1943. A second unaltered edition was published at Tübingen in 1957 (third unaltered edition, 1967).
2   C.H. Cornill, "Ein Elohistischer Bericht über die Entstehung des israelitischen Königthums in I Samuelis i-xv aufgezeigt", Zeitschrift für kirkliche Wissenschaft und kirkliches Leben, 6, 1885, pp.113ff.; "Zur Quellenkritik der Bücher Samuelis", Königsberger Studien I, 1887, pp.25ff.; "Noch einmal Sauls Königswahl und Verwerfung", Zeitschrift für die Alttestamentliche Wissenschaft, 10, 1890, pp.96ff.; K. Budde, Die Bücher Richter und Samuel. Ihre Quellen und ihr Aufbau, 1890.

3   I. Benzinger, Jahwist und Elohist in den Königsbüchern, Beiträge zur Wissenschaft vom Alten und Neuen Testament, 27, 1921.

4   O. Eissfeldt, Die Quellen des Richterbuches, 1925 and his Die Komposition der Samuelisbücher, 1931. See also his later The Old Testament: An Introduction (ET from the 3rd German edition 1964), Oxford 1965.

5   G. Hölscher, Das Buch der Könige, seine Quellen und seine Redaktion, Forschungen zur Religion und Literatur des Alten und Neuen Testaments, 36, 1923.

6   G. Fohrer, Introduction to the Old Testament, London 1970 (ET from the German edition, Heidelberg 1965).

7   R. Kittel, in Die Heilige Schrift des Alten Testaments, 4th edition, ed. A. Bertholet, 1922-23, pp.367ff.

8   L. Rost, Die Überlieferung von der Thronnachfolge Davids, Beiträge zur Wissenschaft vom Alten und Neuen Testament, III:6, 1926 (reprinted in his Das kleine Credo und andere Studien zum alten Testament, Heidelberg 1965, pp.119-253).

9   M. Noth, Das Buch Josua, Tübingen 1938.

10   M. Noth, Das System der zwölf Stämme Israels, Beiträge zur Wissenschaft vom Alten und Neuen Testament, IV:1, 1930.

11   So, for example, O. Eissfeldt in his Introduction referred to in note 4. For a survey see E. Jenni, "Zwei Jahrzehnte Forschung an den Büchern Josua bis Könige", Theologische Rundschau 27, 1961/2, pp.1-32, 97-146.

12   R. Smend, "Das Gesetz und die Völker. Ein Beitrag zur deuteronomistischen Redaktionsgeschichte", in H.W. Wolff (ed.), Probleme Biblischer Theologie, München 1971, pp.494ff.; W. Richter, Die Bearbeitung des "Retterbuches" in der deuteronomischen Epoche, Bonner Biblische Beiträge 21, 1964; W. Dietrich, Prophetie und Geschichte. Eine redaktionsgeschichtliche Untersuchung zum deuteronomistischen Geschichtswerk, Forschungen zur Religion und Literatur des Alten und Neuen Testaments, 108, 1972.

13   F.M. Cross, "The Structure of the Deuteronomic History", in Perspectives in Jewish Learning, vol. III, Chicago 1967, pp.9ff. A similar view is advocated by R.D. Nelson, The Redactional Duality of the Deuteronomistic History (Diss. Union Theological Seminary, Virginia), Xerox University Microfilms, Ann Arbor, Michigan, 1974, which also provides an extensive survey of the debate on this issue, including its nineteenth century background. [A revised version of R.D. Nelson's work is to be published as JSOT Supplement Series, 18.]

Chapter One
THE TASK BEFORE US

The whole of the historical tradition in the Old Testament is contained in a few large compilations. These works have collated and systematised the extremely diverse material of traditional tales and historical reports and enclosed them in a framework, determined in each case by their own particular concerns. Therefore, whoever wishes to investigate the individual elements of this historical tradition, and further, to examine the historical sources critically, and finally, to work towards an account of the history of the Israelite people based on the source material, must first construct for himself an exact picture of the extent and nature of these collections and of the degree to which they have re-worked the older, traditional material, or, at least, have coloured it in some special way by insertions into a particular passage. Only then can the development of the historical tradition itself be clarified.

These great compilations are the Pentateuch and the historical works of the Deuteronomist and of the Chronicler. Among these, the Pentateuch holds a special position. It is true that a large amount of historical stories and reports have found their way into the Pentateuch; however, once its real intentions have been recognised, it cannot be described unreservedly as a compilation, since the subject matter concerns specific themes, fundamental for faith, which are developed - by using numerous historical details. Collating extant traditions was not, therefore, the primary motivation. Rather, it was a question of presenting the foundations of faith and of life /1/ - and this is equally true of the individual "sources", which were later brought together to form the biblical text as we now know it. In view of its particular nature and remembering that the literary and factual analysis of the Pentateuch has already been attempted from many points of view and has reached more or less definite conclusions, the Pentateuch will be left on one side in what follows /2/.

In the works of the Deuteronomist and the Chronicler we have compilations in the strict sense of historical traditions, each work with its own purpose and particular point of view.

1

Thus, these two works are, generally speaking, very closely related to each other. Further, there is the fact that the Chronicler used the Deuteronomist's work as a source and, moreover, as a model. It need not be stressed that the Deuteronomistic work has an outstanding significance as the first collection and editing of historical traditions within Old Testament literature. It marks the beginning of a special type of Biblical literature /3/. Furthermore, it is only within this work that an abundance of priceless, old historical tales and reports are preserved; later these were transferred in part into the Chronicler's history, but were partially distorted and deformed in the process. Without the Deuteronomistic work and the traditional material it absorbed, our knowledge of Israelite history would be pitifully small.

It is obvious, therefore, that an accurate analysis of the Deuteronomistic work is our urgent and important task; once it is completed, a comparable study of the Chronicler's work can be undertaken. The importance of such a task on the Deuteronomist's work in the first instance arises from the fact that this work must first be "discovered" as a literary entity and unity. The Chronicler's work has been handed down as a separate entity and the fact that the end of this work lies in the book of Ezra/Nehemiah, which were not separated from it until later, is so obvious and is, therefore, so generally accepted that we need not devote any further space to the work's external form. Only the question of the correct distinction between original material and secondary expansions need be dealt with once more. Only after determining its original form, can we then define the salient points concerning the presuppositions and intentions of the Chronistic compilation; thereafter some comments can be made concerning the policy which the writer followed in sifting and editing the traditional material.

All these tasks lie before us also in our analysis of the Deuteronomistic work. In this case, though, we must first take the preliminary step of determining its contents, distributed as they are throughout a series of Old Testament "books". Here we are less interested in examining once again which separate elements are "Deuteronomistic" and which are not; the literary-critical foundation was laid long ago and has produced generally accepted conclusions. However, these Deuteronomistic sections have to be examined as a whole. In various cases these sections have proved to be elements of a Deuteronomistic framework that encompasses older traditions. The question should be posed, whether they do not present us with a unity. Thus we must ask, for the whole, the question that has already been answered for the individual parts: do we in fact have here a comprehensive framework indicating a large literary unit which has adopted much traditional material? It will be shown that we should certainly answer this question in the affirmative. We shall therefore find a large collection of traditional material - the work of the Deuteronomist - whose extent and character can consequently be determined more exactly. Such a conclusion could then be the end of the matter if, when it is tested, it should prove clearly correct. But the investigation of the great Deuteronomistic work deserves and demands to be pursued to all its logical conclusions, especially since much of the results of previous literary-critical work must be seen in quite a new light. Therefore, one should not shirk the effort required to follow the author's programme step by step throughout the whole work. Only then will a concrete picture of this important literary work evolve, a work which extends over a massive part of the whole Old Testament. In this way, the thesis that this great work is independent and unified will finally prove justified.

Section A

THE STRUCTURE OF THE WORK AS A WHOLE

Chapter Two
EVIDENCE THAT THE WORK IS A SELF-CONTAINED WHOLE

One of the most conclusive and least disputed findings of scholarly literary criticism is that in the books of Joshua, Judges, 1 and 2 Samuel and 1 and 2 Kings we are confronted with the activity of a Deuteronomistic author in passages both large - sometimes very small. Like all the other historical books in the Old Testament, this author's work is anonymous, but we call him the "Deuteronomistic" author because his language and way of thinking closely resemble those found in the Deuteronomic Law and in the admonitory speeches which precede and follow the Law. Broadly following present academic practice, we shall refer below to this author and his work by the abbreviation Dtr. /1/.

It is generally considered that Dtr. is by a single "Deuteronomistic editor", or rather by different "Deuteronomistic editors" closely resembling one another in their style, and that the nature of their work was to adapt, to some extent, something which had already come into being as a comprehensive narrative complex or as various lengthy narrative complexes. This narrative is represented by the older traditional material found in the individual books mentioned above. It is thought that this adaptation, sometimes more and sometimes less thorough, was intended to highlight certain aspects of the traditional material by means of a clearly defined and strongly emphasised theological interpretation of history. In order to examine the work of Dtr. more closely, let us postpone for the moment considering collections of the traditional material, and let us confine ourselves, for the time being, to the books from Joshua to Kings in which Dtr. is most conspicuous, though not always to the same extent, and let us survey the material attributable to Dtr. To do this we had better ignore, to begin with, the usual division of this historical complex into "books", for this was undoubtedly a secondary process in the history of the tradition and closer investigation is required before we can decide whether it took place before or after Dtr.

The isolation of a "Deuteronomistic" stratum in the books mentioned above has been carried out on the basis of linguistic details. The linguistic evidence remains the most reliable basis for attributing parts of the various traditions to Dtr. The language of Dtr. is very straightforward and dispenses with any particular artistry or refinement; it is the simplest Hebrew in the Old Testament. The limited variety of expression has led to frequent repetition of the same simple phrases and sentence constructions, in which the "Deuteronomistic" style is easily recognised. The characteristics of this style, its vocabulary, diction and sentence structure are, therefore, undisputed; we need not consider them in detail. But we note that this linguistic uniformity in itself must at least suggest that the work is self-contained, even if the absence of specific stylistic peculiarities means that we cannot rely too heavily on this.

To assess the work as a whole, it is more important to notice certain aspects of the arrangement of the books Joshua - Kings which can be traced back to the work of Dtr. In particular, at all the important points in the course of the history, Dtr. brings forward the leading personages with a speech, long or short, which looks forward and backward in an attempt to interpret the course of events, and draws the relevant practical conclusions about what people should do. For example, at the very beginning of Jos. 1, after the introductory words of Yahweh to him, Joshua briefly addresses the Transjordanian tribes in front of all the tribes of Israel; he briefly outlines the task of occupation of the land that lies before them west of the Jordan /2/. Most important, after the Israelites have occupied the land, Dtr. has Joshua, in Jos. 23, make a long, solemn speech to the gathered tribes. In this he formulates the most important instructions for behaviour in the land they have now come to possess. By means of this speech, the course of the narrative moves into the period of the "judges". And as with the transition from this "judges" period to the Kings period, Dtr. marks it with a quite lengthy speech by Samuel in 1 Sam. 12 /3/. In it are presented to the gathering of the people the lessons to be learnt from the vicissitudes of history hitherto and, once again, it is concluded by an admonition to the people concerning their future. Finally, after the completion of the temple in Jerusalem - an event that was of fundamental importance to Dtr.'s theological interpretation of history /4/ -

King Solomon makes a detailed speech in the form of a prayer to God, which thoroughly expounds the significance of the new sanctuary for the present, and especially for the future (1 Kings 8:14ff.). Elsewhere the summarising reflections upon history which sum up the action are presented by Dtr. himself as part of the narrative, whether because they did not lend themselves to reproduction in speeches or because there were not suitable historical figures to make the speeches. Such is the case in Jos. 12 concerning the results of the occupation of the land, and in the programmatic statement for the book of Judges in Judg. 2:11ff.; this presents an anticipatory survey of the cyclical nature of the course of history in the "judges" period in a manner which is quite understandable within the limits of Dtr.'s point of view. Similarly the writer appends to the story of the end of the Israelite state a retrospective reflection upon the grim outcome of the monarchic period in Israel and Judah (2 Kings 17:7ff.). This practice of inserting general retrospective and anticipatory reflections at certain important points in the history has no exact parallels in the Old Testament outside Dtr. Here, then, we have a characteristic which strongly supports the thesis that Dtr. was conceived as a unified and self-contained whole.

Further, the passages discussed above contain the elements of a simple and unified theological interpretation of history and therefore they have much in common with each other in their subject matter. We shall discuss this in greater detail below (pp.89ff.). Here we merely draw attention to the recurring emphasis on obeying the "voice" of God, which manifests itself by making specific demands upon human conduct, and to the lack, conspicuous everywhere, even in 1 Kings 8, of all positive interest in cult practices, and the concern throughout to depict and interpret the historical process showing clearly how God's retributive activity takes its course against the whole people.

At present there is much talk of two stages of "Deutero-nomistic" composition /5/ in the books from Joshua to Kings, and hence Dtr. is not regarded as a unity. This view is based upon (i) the perfectly correct observation that in various places - we shall go into this in detail - Dtr.'s work was subsequently added to in the same style; but this does not disprove the unity of the original Dtr.; (ii) a too early dating of the original "composition" of Dtr. which compels one to ascribe certain passages, which were obviously composed later, to a second Deuteronomistic author /6/. Other arguments against the unity

6

of Dtr.'s work, raised by W. Rudolph /7/, are that the
Deuteronomistic conclusion of Joshua must be sharply
contrasted, both in style and in subject matter, with the
introduction to Judges, that a book of Joshua edited by a
Deuteronomistic writer was originally followed by a separate
Deuteronomistic book of Judges, and that the two books were
joined by a later author who also made the end of Joshua run on
into the beginning of Judges. Rudolph brackets with the
"Deuteronomistic" end of Joshua, Jos. 23 and Judg. 2:6-10,
13,20-22; 3:1a,3,4,6 and puts Judg. 1:1-2,5,23; 3:5; 2:11,12,14-16,
18-19 in the Deuteronomistic introduction to Judges. Thereby,
he allocates virtually all the traditional material between Jos.
23 and Judg. 3:6 to two separate strands /8/. He arrives at this
result firstly by observations of a literary nature - concerning
doublets and other formal inconsistencies - but mainly by an
argument related to subject matter: that the first set of
passages does not let the moral decline set in until after the
death of Joshua's generation and finds those peoples who were
not expelled on the border of the area occupied by the Israelite
tribes, whereas, according to the second set of passages, the
Joshua generation were already beginning to forsake God and
some of the pre-Israelite inhabitants of Palestine had stayed
within Israelite territory. It seems to me that Rudolph's
proposal is primarily intended to clear up the literary
complexities of Judg. 2:11-3:6. But even in this he fails to
convince; for it is very hard to discover the elements of two
independent and self-contained literary units in Judg. 2:11-3:6
/9/ - rather, analysis shows a "Deuteronomistic" foundation
which is augmented in various ways by secondary sources. As
early as Judg. 2:11b,12,13 we have three (not two) parallel
sentences which say the same thing and display the same
"Deuteronomistic" style. Here then, variants, composed with
the "Deuteronomistic" expressions familiar elsewhere, were
subsequently annexed to the original text /10/, just as in
v.15a^b - which Rudolph does not discuss - two synonymous
variants appear side by side. An actual example of a secondary
expansion to the text is the whole section telling how the
foreign peoples stayed in Israelite territory (Judg. 2:20-3:6) /11/
- this is not motivated in its context, it already presupposes the
additions in Jos. 23 and the existence of Judg. 1:21,27ff. and it
is not consistent in itself. Anyone who disputes this judgement
of the passage and prefers to put it in the same category as
2:11-19 must still admit that an uncontrived explanation of its

7

literary difficulties would suggest not two parallel threads, but rather a basic core augmented by secondary sources. After the introductory verses (2:20-21), which explain the foreign nations' continuing presence in the promised land as an expression of divine wrath and hence a punishment for the unfaithful Israelite tribes, v.22 assumes the existence of (2:20-21) but immediately brings in the idea of "temptation" by the foreign nations still in the area - this shows that v.22 is, in both style and subject matter, the work of a secondary author. But 3:1a,3,4 /12/ are very closely linked with 2:22 /13/. The other basic elements of this section on the foreign peoples are Judg. 2:20,21 /14/ and 3:5-6. I cannot think of Judg. 2:11-3:6 as a mere juxtaposition of two parallel Deuteronomistic threads. But the main stumbling block in Rudolph's thesis is his untenable evaluation of Judg. 1; he claims that this chapter is the beginning of the Deuteronomistic introduction to Judges, assuming that the "Deuteronomistic editor" of Judges took over the old, traditional material present in Judg. 1 and used it to illustrate his idea that the foreign peoples stayed in the territory of the Israelite tribes. Now, it is generally recognised that Judg. 1 shows no signs of Deuteronomistic editing. The method of Dtr. as we know it makes it quite unthinkable that Judg. 1 was part of a Deuteronomistic framework; and this is the point at issue. Without Judg. 1 the Deuteronomistic material in the section Jos. 23:1-Judg. 3:6 is not substantial enough to be allocated to two independent Deuteronomistic frameworks. Rather - and this is the positive conclusion to be drawn from the discussion above - the speech by Joshua with which Dtr. ends his account of the Conquest (Jos. 23) is directly linked with the transition, also composed by Dtr., to the history of the period of the "judges", set forth in Judg. 2:6-11,14-16,18-19 /15/. Afterwards, in the style similar to that of Dtr., the Deuteronomistically edited passages Jos. 24:1-28 /16/ and Judg. 2:1-5 were added after the final chapter of the book of Joshua, chapter 23, and - later still - without any Deuteronomistic revision, the mass of old traditional fragments, which form the present Judg. 1 /17/.

Rudolph's argument required this detailed treatment because, so far as I can see, we have here the only exhaustive attempt to use techniques of literary criticism to prove the co-existence of independent "Deuteronomistic redactions" for the separate, individual, biblical books. Furthermore, it is only at the point where Joshua ends and Judges begins that such an attempt must be undertaken and tested; in any case, we must ask ourselves here whether Dtr. is self-contained. As far as stages of "Deuteronomistic editing" are concerned, the transitions between Judges and Samuel and between Samuel and Kings is so smooth and clear that we can assume without further ado that Dtr. wrote it all. Now we have found that this assumption also applies to the transition from Joshua to Judges. This may suggest that Dtr. was not familiar with the division of the source material into the "books" Joshua-Kings, for every passage between Jos. 23 and Judg. 2:6 which points to a division between Joshua and Judges was brought in after Dtr., and the same is true of the passages at the end of Judges and 2 Samuel. The suggestion is confirmed if we consider that Dtr. arranged the material differently from the way the later books did. If we are right to suppose that Dtr. organised the traditional material systematically by inserting speeches of anticipation and retrospection, delivered by the protagonists, then (i) he probably ended his account of the period of conquest with Jos. 23 - the end of the book of Joshua as edited by a "Deuteronomistic writer"; (ii) he ended his account of the "judges" period with Samuel's speech in 1 Sam. 12 - long after the end of the book of Judges; and (iii) he concluded his account of the first part of the monarchic period with Solomon's building of the temple, which is marked in 1 Kings 8:14ff. by Solomon's prayer of dedication of the Temple.

We conclude, then, for the present, that Dtr., using material from the tradition, planned the history of his people in Joshua-Kings in accordance with a unified plan and divided it according to subject matter.

The unity of Dtr. becomes apparent only if we look at the material which he used from the old tradition; for this material is very diverse in every respect. We have the traditional material on the conquest of land in the first half of Joshua /18/, much of which is compiled from popular aetiological traditions, and the long, coherent and historical accounts in 1 and 2 Samuel; we also have the equally varied stories of individual heroes in Judges and the stories about the prophets in Kings. And these are only the more conspicuous elements. All these sections differ greatly from one another in style, manner, intention and source, quite unlike the parts composed by a "Deuteronomistic writer" which are uniform throughout the work. The unity of the latter is the more obvious because it stands in contrast to the diversity of the older material. We must stress above all that the pre-Deuteronomistic material shows no intrinsic continuity in Joshua-Kings; rather we must account for its coherence by assuming a "Deuteronomistic editor". It is only in short passages that we have any evidence of pre-Deuteronomistic compilation of individual traditions; e.g. in Jos. 2ff. we have popular traditions compiled to make the story of the settlement, and extended writings on Saul and David were linked with one another. Between the separate stories in Judges, however, there is no evidence of pre-Deuteronomistic cohesion /19/, and it is generally recognised that the same is true of the separate sections, of varying lengths, on the kings of Israel and Judah, which are held together only by the work of Dtr. with their chronological framework. Over and above this, however, Dtr. is wholly responsible for the coherence of this complex of material and hence the unity of the whole history in Joshua-Kings which is clearly intentional as is shown by the form of these books as we have it.

Scholars have failed to draw the one possible conclusion from these findings. This is due to the fact that the way in which techniques of literary criticism have been applied to all the narrative books in the Old Testament has invariably been heavily influenced by the critical work done on the "Hexateuch". From this starting point, the critics have always looked for connections in old, pre-Deuteronomistic sources /20/ and thus could allow the "Deuteronomistic editor" nothing but a secondary and inessential role in the construction of the work /21/. But it is clear that the literary conditions in the "Hexateuch" cannot be transferred to the later books without reservation. The most obvious reservation is that there is no "Deuteronomistic editing" in Genesis-Numbers. If we take the perfectly sound approach of interpreting the relatively simple and clear conditions in Joshua-Kings, without regard to the findings of literary criticism elsewhere, and postpone discussing the very controversial "Hexateuch" questions in their application to Joshua, we can reach only one conclusion:

Dtr. was not merely an editor but the author of a history which brought together material from highly varied traditions and arranged it according to a carefully conceived plan. In general Dtr. simply reproduced the literary sources available to him and merely provided a connecting narrative for isolated passages. We can prove, however, that in places he made a deliberate selection from the material at his disposal /22/. As far as facts were concerned, the elements were arranged as given in tradition - e.g. the whole of the history of the kings, or the insertion of the period of the "judges" between the occupation of the land and the period of the monarchy. At times the order is determined by the older tradition, as in the incidents prior to the conquest. Elsewhere, though, Dtr. apparently arranged the material according to his own judgement, as in the details of the history of the "judges". Thus Dtr.'s method of composition is very lucid. The closest parallels are those Hellenistic and Roman historians who use older accounts, mostly unacknowledged, to write a history not of their own time but of the more or less distant past.

Chapter Three
THE BEGINNING OF THE HISTORY

Dtr.'s history reaches a natural conclusion at the end of 2 Kings with the actual end of the history of the kings of Israel and Judah, the destruction of the nations of Israel and Judah. Admittedly, at the very end, 2 Kings 25:27-30, Dtr. goes on to report that king Jehoiachin was freed by the Babylonian king Amel-Marduk, but this is only to provide a mitigating conclusion to the long account of the decline which Dtr. had to give, not to conceal or leave in doubt the fact that the history of the Israelite and Judaean kings was in fact over. At the same time, this concluding observation concerns an event of 562 B.C., and this gives us a definite terminus a quo for the date of Dtr.'s work. We have no reason to put Dtr. much later than this terminus a quo. On the other hand we have just as little reason to apply this terminus a quo to a second stage of "Deutero-nomistic editing" rather than to Dtr.'s activity as a whole; for all parts of Dtr. which point to an earlier date of composition belong, as we shall demonstrate in detail, to the old material adapted by Dtr. The history of Dtr. was written, then, around the middle of the sixth century B.C. when the history of the Israelite people in the original sense was essentially at an end.

It seems harder to decide what point marks the beginning of Dtr. At any rate, Jos. 1 is certainly not the beginning: the links of this chapter with the Moses story and, in particular, the account of the settlement of some tribes in Transjordan, show that these matters have already been treated in Dtr.'s work. But how far back did Dtr. go? It is generally assumed that Dtr.'s history began with the Creation /1/. This depends on the customary view of the Deuteronomistic activity as a stage in the literary development of the "Hexateuch", a stage which simply extended into the later historical books. The old pre-Deuteronomistic sources of the "Hexateuch" are regarded as the essential core of the narrative tradition throughout the Old Testament and, from this viewpoint, everything else looks like an imitation, continuation, or later adaptation of the "Hexateuchal" sources. Thus, if Dtr. took over and unified old material, he must have included the old "Hexateuchal" sources.

Now the view that Dtr. started with the book of Genesis is

obviously mistaken, for it is generally recognised that there is no sign of "Deuteronomistic editing" in Genesis-Numbers /2/. Now, even where he took over the long passages of continuous narrative which already existed, in the same way as the old "Hexateuchal" sources are normally believed to have been taken over and worked into a single unit, Dtr. still expands and augments his material, with longer or shorter additions, in order to express his particular viewpoint, quite apart from his tendency to insert extensive reflections at important points in the narrative. He does this with the old conquest story in the first part of Joshua, where he inserts and reworks the whole section, as well as with the old Saul-David material /3/ which he took over as a unified complex. In the old "Hexateuchal" narrative he would have had every opportunity for similar editorial intervention. Given that the books Genesis-Numbers show no signs of such an adaptation by Dtr. and that these books, therefore, look completely different from Joshua-Kings, we can only conclude that the books Genesis-Numbers, or at any rate the form of these books that antedated the Priestly Work, were not part of Dtr.'s work.

We must look, then, to Deuteronomy (Deut.) for the beginning of Dtr.'s work. In Deut. 31:1-13 and in parts of Deut. 34 we have, in fact, for the first time the elements of a Deuteronomistic narrative with which Joshua 1 is directly linked. Here Moses takes his leave of the people, says that they are to take possession of the land west of the Jordan, appoints Joshua as his successor, and finally dies. In this context, Moses mentions "this law" (Deut. 31:9-13) meaning the Deuteronomic law, and so it is obvious that the whole of the Deuteronomic law and its framework are part of Dtr.'s narrative. This assumption is justifiably widely accepted since the content of the law is demonstrably of fundamental importance for Dtr.'s view of history, and Dtr.'s language adopts the patterns of that used in this law and its framework. Does this mean that Dtr. started his history with the account of the proclamation of the Deuteronomic law by Moses? This, like other interpretations, does not quite fit the facts of the case. If, bearing in mind the scope and independence of Dtr.'s historical work, one looks closely at what are commonly called the introductory speeches in the Deuteronomic law, one quickly finds persuasive evidence that the first of these introductory speeches, Deut. 1:1-4:43 /4/, has nothing particular in common with the Deuteronomic law but is directly related to the Deuteronomistic history.

From this we conclude that Deut. 1-3(4) is not the introduction to the Deuteronomic law but the beginning of the Deuteronomistic historical narrative and that this narrative begins therefore at Deut. 1:1. For one thing, Deut. 31:1ff., that is, the beginning of Dtr.'s narrative <u>after</u> the communication of Dt. (the Deuteronomic law and its admonitory framework), is directly linked in language and subject matter to Deut. 3:23-29, that is (leaving aside Deut. 4:1-40 [41-43] which is a special case), to the end of the introductory piece by Dtr. before the communication of the Deuteronomic law together with its framework. Our conclusion is supported, in particular, by the fact that here the history of the Mosaic period does not seem intended to illustrate various admonitions and warnings, as, at times, in Deut. 5-11, but rather is obviously narrated out of interest in the reported events themselves. This point is perfectly clear if one stops trying to interpret Deut. 1-3 as one of the introductory speeches to the Deuteronomic law. We may add that the available material on the history of the period of "wandering" in Deut. 1-3 is obviously selected /5/ to supply the needs of Dtr.'s work, that is, the accent here is on matters which are relevant to the developments to be narrated by Dtr. later and which are necessary if the reader is to understand the later account. This explains the detailed reference (in 2:26ff., before Deut. 3:23-29 which anticipates the death of Moses and his replacement by Joshua) to the defeat of the two Amorite kings Sihon and Og in Transjordan, to the occupation of their territories, and to the allocation of these to the tribes of Reuben and Gad and the half-tribe of Manasseh on the condition that they take part in the conquest of the land west of the Jordan; for in Jos. 1 knowledge of these events is expressly presupposed. Indeed, as many allusions in his work suggest, and as we know, Dtr. is the source of the belief that the conquest should be divided into two parallel strands, that of the occupation of the east bank under Moses and that of the west bank by Joshua; but only the latter of these is related in detail on the basis of an existing and extensive tradition. The Israelite conquest is indirectly related, also, to the earlier, longer section of Moses' introductory speech (Deut. 2:1-25). This section indicates (as is repeatedly and deliberately emphasised at all opportunities) that the Israelites will win nothing /6/ from the territories of the Edomites, Moabites and Ammonites, through or by which the tribes must pass. At the same time, this section is a link-passage, necessary for continuity, to join what goes before with what comes after. But it is preceded by Deut. 1:19-46, the story of the spies, which is similarly told in some detail; this story is directly relevant to the narrative of the occupation of Palestine, because it explains why arable Palestine was occupied not from the south but from the east, and above all lays the groundwork for the Caleb story which occurs in Jos. 14:6-14 /7/. The sections of Moses' speech discussed hitherto display a definite thematic unity and we need not furnish detailed proof that these are not just excerpts from the old "Hexateuchal" sources in Numbers but rather anticipate throughout not, it is true, the Deuteronomic law but, at any rate, the conquest story given in Joshua, and tell us what we need to know to understand it. But just before this part of Deut. comes Deut. 1:9-18, a short passage on the appointment of various leaders, officers and judges for the Israelite tribes. This does not look like a necessary part of the whole, even though the Deuteronomic law mentions "judges and officers" (Deut. 16:18 and passim) and more important, Jos. 1:10 and 3:2 assume the existence of "officers". Perhaps we do better to relate the subject matter of this passage to the introduction to the speech by Moses - Deut. 1:6-8 - which is about the departure from Horeb and could easily lead into an observation on the organisation of the tribes who were then wandering in the desert. The actual introduction to Moses' speech, which looks back to the Israelite tribes' stay at Horeb, can easily be explained by the need to introduce the whole work by mentioning a prominent event.

Why does Dtr. make the whole of this narrative take the form of a speech by Moses? Clearly the main purpose was the communication of the Deuteronomic law, which was of such fundamental importance to him. Now it was already established in the passages serving as a framework to the law (cf. in particular Deut. 8:2ff.) that Moses did not proclaim it until the end of the period of wandering through the desert. Therefore, before reporting the law, Dtr. had to summarise briefly those events of the period of wandering of which knowledge was required in order to understand his subsequent narrative. But we have shown that elsewhere he liked to put such summaries in the form of speeches by leading characters. Furthermore, the Deuteronomic law itself existed in the form of a speech by Moses and within the framework of speeches by Moses, so that Dtr. only needed to precede Moses' speech introducing the law with a fairly long prologue recalling earlier history to fulfil all requirements /8/.

The Deuteronomic law as taken over by Dtr. had essentially the same form as we know today in Deut. 4:44-30:20. This is shown in particular by the fact that Dtr. assumes knowledge of one of the most subsidiary elements in the framework of the Deuteronomic law, that is, Deut. 27:1-8, for, relying on Deut. 27:1-8, Dtr. went on to incorporate Jos. 8:30-35 into the established tradition of the occupation of the land. But because the literary growth of the original Deuteronomic law to its present extent (Deut. 4:44-30:20) must be dated before Dtr., we should allow an interval between the Deuteronomic law and Dtr.; this only confirms what has been said above (p.12). This also absolves us from the need to consider the literary history of the Deuteronomic law in further detail at this point, but let us indicate briefly the conclusions to be drawn from the fact that Deut. 1-3(4) is not part of the framework of the Deuteronomic law.

This fact essentially does no more than confirm a thesis which has already been proved conclusively in my opinion by G. Hölscher /9/: the extant literary material cannot support the common assumption /10/, that there was a series of "special editions" of the Deuteronomic law, each of which may be taken to represent a stage in the composition of the framework of the law. Such an assumption is implausible because of the contrived and complicated literary processes which it presupposes. If the Deuteronomic law does not start until Deut. 4:44, as suggested above, it becomes abundantly clear that the traditional material of the Deuteronomic law simply accumulated from all manner of additions to an original basic core. If we see the original core in the passages with singular addressees - and this thesis has surely established itself as correct - then the passages with plural addressees, not only in the law but also in the introductory speech (Deut. 4:44-11:32) /11/, are shown to be essentially unconnected additions. In the secondary prefatory speech, Deut. 5, the whole Deuteronomic law is explained, after the fact, as an exposition of the Decalogue proclaimed at Horeb, which Moses received from God at Horeb but did not present to the people until the end of their wandering. Here we should note that the Decalogue which was written on stone tablets - as we are told here for the first time in no uncertain terms (v.19) - together with its subsequent explanation in the Deuteronomic law by Moses, is declared to be the only divine guidance given to the people at Horeb. Furthermore, between

Deut. 9:7a and 10:10ff., there is a more extensive addition with
plural addressees ("you" form). This illustrates the statement in
9:7a that the people in the desert provoked their God to wrath,
by giving a detailed account of their apostasy to worship the
"golden calf", and is, therefore, seen to be not part of an
independent narrative, but rather dependent on the basic core
with its singular addressee /12/. Finally Deut. 11:16-32 is a
series of disconnected additions in the first of which the theme
at the beginning of the introductory speech with singular
addressee is elaborated by a later hand which makes particular
use of the statements in Deut. 6:7-9. These additions have no
claim to be considered parts of a self-contained introductory
speech in the "you" form. If the self-contained passage Deut.
1-3(4) is no longer seen as an introductory speech to the
Deuteronomic law but rather as the introduction to Dtr., then
we have no more cause to suppose parallel introductory
speeches to the Deuteronomic law. The same applies to the
concluding speeches where, in any case, there is little to be said
for assuming parallel strands. Here, the basic material, with
singular addressee ("thou" form), in Deut. 27:9-10 + *28:1-68 +
*30:15-20, seems to have been augmented first by the word of
comfort, 30:1-4, expressed with singular addressee and motivated by the state of exile. Meanwhile, we have unconnected
expansion in the instruction of 27:1-8, which lacks inner unity,
further in the collection of twelve curses, with their
introduction, in 27:11-26, and finally the long threatening
speech, 28:69-29:28, which addresses an audience in the plural,
and in the introduction to this we have the first and only
instance of the idea of a covenant "in the land of Moab" as
opposed to the Horeb covenant. It is now usually assumed that
this successive growth, particularly of the framework passages,
resulted from the practice of reading the law aloud and
following it with sermon-like introductory remarks and
expositions. This looks probable enough, but, generally speaking,
it seems to have come to an end once Dtr. incorporated the
Deuteronomic law into his history as the first large-scale
complex of tradition.

Chapter Four
THE CHRONOLOGICAL FRAMEWORK

Dtr. was extremely interested in chronological questions, that is in establishing exactly when, in relation to each other, the events of which he tells took place. This is immediately apparent from the structure of the books of Kings, which is his work, for here continuity is achieved by means of the chronological system, which is based on the reigns of both lines of kings, the length of whose rule is always given, and also on the close links established between the two lines by the attempt to date them in relation to each other. We do not propose to inquire into the sources which Dtr. used for the chronological material, but would note simply that he intended to supply and in fact did supply an unbroken chronology for the period of the Israelite and Judaean monarchies using specific and, as we can show, on the whole reliable sources. If we take even a superficial look at Dtr.'s work in Kings, we find that he is not exclusively interested in evaluating the individual kings and thus, indirectly, the monarchy per se (most scholars lay a one-sided stress on this aspect alone); rather, he is just as interested in constructing a definitive chronology, and for this purpose went to the trouble of taking over and reporting so many individual numbers from his sources.

Moreover, the same chronological interest is shown in the parts of Dtr. dealing with the pre-monarchic history of the Israelite people. Let us pose the question here, what kind of sources were available to Dtr. for his chronological data. We can in any case be certain that, here too, Dtr. meant to provide an unbroken chronology. Admittedly, the sources at his disposal gave no coherent account of this earlier period such as was available for the monarchic period and, as we shall show, he was forced in places to close the gaps in the tradition himself, apparently by inserting his own round numbers. At any rate, this consistent interest in chronology is a further proof that Dtr. is a single author and his work self-contained.

Now, at one point, Dtr. sums up the whole chronology of the pre-monarchic period in a specific figure and thereby links it firmly to the chronology of the monarchic period. The information in 1 Kings 6:1, generally and rightly attributed to a

18

"Deuteronomistic editor", is that the fourth year of Solomon's reign was also the four hundred and eightieth year after the Israelites" exodus from Egypt - this is the year in which Solomon "built the temple for Yahweh". We must test our statement that Dtr. is a single author and his work self-contained in the light of chronological information, by asking if the figure of 480 is consistent with the chronological data in Deuteronomy-Samuel. We must first ask what could have caused Dtr. to sum up the chronology in this way at this point, and at this point only in his work. Surely he does so, in the first place, because of the significance of the building of the temple by Solomon for Dtr.'s view of history /1/ - this also prompted him to insert the long prayer of dedication in 1 Kings 8:14ff. This for Dtr. was a milestone in history. But we must also note that, for one reason or another, Dtr. was in a position to state the impressive round number 480. Let us disregard the question of whether Dtr. was here indulging in numerological speculation or contemplating a general periodisation of history extending across the historical events narrated in his work. Any meaning behind this figure is more or less a mystery which we can no longer solve with any certainty; however, there is no compelling reason to look for any such meaning. Even those who cannot resist assuming that this figure has a particular "significance" must admit that Dtr. had to relate this figure explicitly to the chronological data he has given elsewhere for the specific historical period in question. But perhaps the simplest and most likely explanation is the following: for the time from the start of Dtr. - for the visit of the Israelite tribes to Horeb, with which the narrative of Dtr. begins, was certainly placed near in time to the Exodus, even in the same year /2/ - to the important event of the building of the temple, the round number 480 more or less emerged of itself from the dates given in Deuteronomy-Samuel, mostly adopted from earlier accounts and only in the occasional passage calculated by Dtr. himself; then Dtr., with his chronological interest, would certainly have had in view the sum total of the dates he had given, and, therefore, understandably enough, drew deliberate attention to this important fact (1 Kings 6:1). Then the fact that Dtr. gives only one such all-embracing date in his history could be easily explained: this was the only time when such a round sum total made up of the separate periods emerged "by chance" /3/.

We must examine the relationship of the 480 years mentioned in 1 Kings 6:1 to the sum total of the individual figures given

for the period from Moses to Solomon. Let us start with the
chronology of the "judges" period, since the situation here
seems the most complicated. Here matters have been confused
by the view of the chronology in Judges put forward by
Wellhausen /4/, subsequently altered /5/ and finally utterly
rejected /6/ by him, but faithfully re-adopted, in particular by
Budde /7/. This view goes together with an equally mistaken
view of the literary development of Judges and, more important
in this context, of the structure of the "Deuteronomistic Book
of Judges". According to this reading, the "Deuteronomistic
Book of Judges" included only the stories of the "major judges"
while the series of "minor judges" with the dates assigned to
them was not included in Judges until much later and therefore
cannot form part of Dtr.'s chronology /8/. It will be shown
conclusively below (pp.42ff.) that Dtr. used both the individual
"major judges" and the series of "minor judges" for his account
of the period and had a very specific reason for relating the two
groups to each other as closely as he does in the book of Judges
as we know it. Furthermore, the fact that Judg. 10:1 is
explicitly linked with Judg. 9 shows that we must count the
story of Abimelech as part of Dtr.'s work, unless we have
recourse to arbitrary hypotheses. Finally, we see partly from
the explicit wording of the text, partly from the attitude of
Dtr., as indicated by his manner of expression, that the figures
given up to Judg. 12:15 /9/ are to be understood as consecutive,
not as concurrent or overlapping. The length of the period of
the "judges", then, is calculated from the various periods during
which foreign enemies ruled the Israelite tribes, together with
the period of "rest" following each act of liberation by a "judge"
and also the periods of office of the "minor judges" which are
inserted in two places between the first two, which otherwise
simply alternate with each other. Dtr. could obviously draw
upon one of the traditions available to him for the exact periods
for the "minor judges" and for the "rule by foreigners", although
it is unclear what kind of source could have supplied the latter
dates. But for the "times of peace" Dtr. can give only round
figures for which he obviously used his own judgement; here the
figure 40 is standard. It is easy to see what 40 means. As we
have said above, it cannot mean the age difference between one
generation and the next, but clearly means the length of time in
which one group of active adult men is completely replaced by
the next /10/; as a rule, none of those who participated in any
given historical event, whether in a position of responsibility or

just aware of what was going on, will be in public life 40 years later. This is made very clear in the statement that the wanderings of the Israelite tribes in the wilderness took 40 years /11/; after this time, all those who reacted to the spies' report are supposed to have died. Dtr. normally lets 40 years elapse between each major act of liberation by one of the "major judges" and the next apostasy of the people, implying what he had made explicit (in Judg. 2:10, in the general introduction to the period of the "judges") about the apostasy after the great events of the period of conquest: in the meanwhile "all that generation /12/ were gathered to their fathers and there arose another generation after them who did not know Yahweh nor the work he had done for Israel".

It should now be easy to determine the length of time Dtr. sees as elapsing between the first apostasy in the period of the "judges" and the death of the last "minor judge" in Judg. 12:15. According to Judg. 3:8,11 the time from the first apostasy and the subsequent oppression by a foreign enemy to the defeat of the enemy and the subsequent time of peace is a total of 8 + 40 = 48 years; the period immediately after is reckoned at 18 (Judg. 3:14) + 80 (3:30) /13/ = 98 years; then we have 20 (Judg. 4:3) + 40 (5:31) = 60 years, and then 7 (6:1) + 40 (8:28) = 47 years. According to Judg. 8:28bff. and 9:1ff. the short episode of Abimelech's reign - 3 years (9:22) - comes immediately after the death of Gideon. According to Judg. 10:1 this is followed immediately by the period of the first two "minor judges", a total of 45 years (Judg. 10:2-3). Next come the 18 years of foreign rule in Judg. 10:8, and this is followed by Jephthah's victory, and then the directly consecutive 15 years period of office of the four "minor judges" given in Judg. 12:7-15 /14/, making a total of 31 years. This brings the time from the first apostasy to the death of the last "minor judge" up to exactly 350 years.

After this things seem to become more complicated; but I think that Dtr.'s intention is clear and unambiguous throughout. When Judg. 13:1 tells us of the 40 years of Philistine rule following the death of the last "minor judge", it goes beyond the scope appropriate to the book of Judges as we know it; this is a further proof that there was no self-contained "Deutero-nomistic Book of Judges" and that where Dtr. mentions the figure 40 in Judg. 13:1 /15/ he has a larger context in mind and not the division into books which we know. For no matter when one wants to date the beginning of Samson's 20 years in office as a "judge" (Judg. 15:20; 16:31), the appearance of Samson, who died a prisoner of the Philistines, has nothing to do with the liberation from the 40 years of Philistine oppression. This liberation clearly does not come about until the Israelites, led by Samuel, defeat the Philistines, as is reported in 1 Sam. 7:7ff. /16/. Within Dtr.'s work, the connection of these events is so unmistakable that the other dates given for the period must be calculated from that time. The result is that we must conclude that we cannot simply add together all the time spans mentioned in this section of the text in its present form. Instead, the writer who put this section into its present form expected a certain amount of overlapping. According to 1 Sam. 7:2, the unsuccessful battle against the Philistines which resulted in the loss of the ark - here Dtr. bases his report on the old ark legend - took place 20 years before the defeat of the Philistines under Samuel /17/, that is, halfway through the 40 years of Philistine rule mentioned in Judg. 13:1. According to 1 Sam. 4:18, Eli, who dies of shock at the news of this defeat, had "judged" Israel for 40 years before his death. This would mean that Eli's term of office goes back through the first half of Philistine rule and Samson's time as "judge" to the time of the last three "minor judges" of Judg. 12:8-15. Several "judges" could hardly have served concurrently. And it is even less permissible to simplify matters by preferring the Septuagint variant in 1 Sam. 4:18, which gives Eli 20 instead of 40 years as a "judge". For it is highly probable that the Septuagint reading is based on a correction by a later hand, which is specifically meant to obviate, at least in part, the difficulties above. We have established that Judg. 13:1 and 1 Sam. 7:7ff. are unquestionably connected. Moreover, one might initially see reason to attribute to Dtr. the interpolation of the chronological information in 1 Sam. 4:18b into the ark legend which he took over from the tradition; but he would be unlikely to complicate his chronology, otherwise so clear and straightforward, in such a strange way, by using a figure of his own making /18/. We must conclude that the dating in 1 Sam. 4:18b was obviously made by a later writer who wanted to incorporate Eli into the line of "judges" as Samuel's predecessor, even though the tradition makes Eli nothing more than priest of the sanctuary of Shiloh, and he is, therefore, not entitled to be incorporated in this way. Furthermore, the interpolation of this figure presupposes the later division of Dtr.'s work into books; the division would mean that no one would notice that the dates of 1 Sam. 4:18b overlapped with those in the book of Judges. So far as Samson is concerned, the suggestion in Judg. 15:20 and 16:31 that he "judged" for 20 years is to be understood as an attempt to fill in the first half of the period of Philistine rule before the events of 1 Sam. 4-6. Admittedly, one may question whether the Samson stories are the work of Dtr. - we shall discuss this further below - and this would make the explanation even simpler. In any case, the figure given in Judg. 13:1 is related to the event reported in 1 Sam. 7:7ff. And so Dtr. calculates the whole period of "judges" from the first apostasy to Samuel's victory over the Philistines as 390 years.

As for the period of Moses and the occupation of the land, Deut. 1:3 tells us that the great speech of Moses in which he proclaims the Deuteronomic law and, hence, his death, occurred in the 40th year /19/. Dtr. says that the conquest of Cisjordan took 5 years; this emerges from Jos. 14:10 which says that 45 years elapsed between the sending of spies into the land of Palestine from Kadesh /20/ and the final allotment of the conquered land among the Israelite tribes /21/. Here Dtr.'s account is simple and unambiguous.

Similarly, the time from Saul's accession to the fourth year of Solomon's reign is fixed by an unbroken chain of data. In 1 Sam. 13:1, the reign of Saul lasted "two years". Admittedly, it is generally thought that this data has been subject to damage at a late stage, or that the whole verse was added by a much later hand. The verse is missing in LXX[B] and several other Septuagint manuscripts, but this means little, given the liberties which the Septuagint takes with the Hebrew text, especially in the "Books of Kingdoms". It would in fact be very surprising if Dtr. with his interest in chronological questions did not give a date for the reign of Saul. 1 Sam. 13:1 was certainly inserted by Dtr. at the appropriate place after 1 Sam. 12 in the style of his formulaic introductions to the reigns of kings elsewhere /22/. But one may object that the figure given for Saul's reign must still be textually corrupt. It is generally considered to be too low to be historically possible. But surely Dtr. could have found the date in some source or other and taken it over in his material on Saul /23/, and apart from that, the figure is certainly not as historically implausible or impossible as people suppose, since Saul's reign was undoubtedly brief /24/. In any case, here we are not trying to establish the chronology of historical events but rather examining the chronological system of Dtr., and there is no solid reason to disregard the date given in 1 Sam. 13:1 /25/. In the concluding passages in 1 Kings 2:11 Dtr. assigns David a reign of 40 years /26/. This brings the time between Saul's accession and the end of the first four years of Solomon's reign to a total of 46 years.

We have now discussed all the relevant figures given by Dtr. and we find that the total time from the exodus out of Egypt to the fourth year of Solomon's reign is 481 years. We cannot say for certain why Dtr. differs from this by a year. But, in adding up his figures, Dtr. has no doubt used the postdating system, as was customary in his time /27/. The most likely explanation may seem to be that, since according to 1 Kings 1:11ff. Solomon was anointed king while David was still alive, Dtr. tacitly identified the last year of David with the first year of Solomon and so made the fourth year of Solomon's reign, already in the tradition as the year in which the temple building began /28/, the 480th year after the exodus.

The fact remains, though, that when Dtr. reaches his total in 1 Kings 6:1, he assumes that his chronological system has no gaps; but the system, closely examined, does have its defects, since there are two short interludes for which Dtr. gives no numerical data and which he simply omits from his final calculation. These are the last stages of Joshua's and Samuel's terms of office. According to Jos. 23:1 and 1 Sam. 7:13b,15,16 and 8:1-2, Joshua was still active, possibly for only a short time, after he completed the final land distribution (before the first apostasy of the Israelite tribes), and the same is true of Samuel after he defeated the Philistines and before the people demanded a king. We can hardly suppose that Dtr. merely overlooked this. More probably, he set the death of Joshua and of the whole generation of the period of the occupation of the land immediately after the distribution of land, which in any case was consistent with the vague wording of Jos. 23:1 /29/. This, of course, he could have done only in order to fit a preconceived chronological system. For the same reason, he omitted to do the obvious thing, that is, to introduce a 40 year period such as was usual in the account of the epoch of the judges /30/; I find this most remarkable. Similarly, one would have expected Dtr. to introduce a 40 year period for Samuel's term as "judge"; there too he refrains from doing so. Perhaps he wanted to show thereby that, just as the facts permit and the text requires the statement in 1 Sam. 7:13b to include the early period of Saul, similarly the figures in 1 Sam. 7:15ff. are meant to include the time after Saul's accession and the time before the defeat of the Philistines; and that the events of 1 Sam. 8:1-2 occupied so little time that the people could have demanded a king within the year immediately following the defeat of the Philistines. The phrasing in the two passages does not make this interpretation natural, but it seems that Dtr. intended such an interpretation when he left out any specific chronological information.

But having seen these two instances in the light of the figure 480 in 1 Kings 6:1, we find that Dtr. had this chronological refinement in mind all along. He did not see 480 as a fabrication; it is founded on the copious information about dates which he found in his sources and used in his work, and on a series of dates - the 40 year periods - which he himself inserted but which spring from the traditional view of the course of history. This number did not, however, emerge of itself, uncontrived, since in two places an artificial conception was necessary to reach the total. This, then, is another proof - and the reason for our detailed consideration of chronology - that Dtr.'s history is a planned self-contained unity and that Dtr. manifestly organised the broad outline and the chronological framework before working out the details. Furthermore, the chronological system shows that the arrangement of the work as a whole, as intended and executed, has nothing to do with the subsequent division of it into "Books". Samuel and Kings are obviously closely linked by a broadly conceived chronology and so are Judges and Samuel. We cannot suppose that they underwent a separate "Deuteronomistic editing" as individual books. The dating in Jos. 14:10 links Deuteronomy and Joshua, and the number 480 in 1 Kings 6:1 encompasses all these "Books". This confirms that Dtr.'s work is a self-contained unit - the view for which we advanced other arguments above (pp.4ff.).

Section B

THE STRUCTURE OF THE PARTS

Now that we have a general view of Dtr.'s history, we must examine the nature of work in detail. We do not need to give a running commentary on the whole work or on those parts formulated by Dtr. himself; rather we must look carefully at the devices Dtr. uses and the attitudes he takes in the process of converting the manifold historical material at his disposal into a unified whole. In this context we need not inquire into the individual origins of the larger complexes of tradition which Dtr. incorporates into his work, but we must continually examine Dtr.'s relation to older forms of the historical tradition.

Chapter Five
THE HISTORY OF THE MOSAIC PERIOD

Dtr. uses a speech by Moses, placed just before the proclamation of the law, to report the historical events between the sojourn of the Israelite tribes at Mount Horeb and the proclamation of the Deuteronomic law at the end of the wanderings in the wilderness. This arrangement may have been prompted by the existence of older more extensive accounts of the period of wandering /1/ so that he needed only to refer, by means of Moses' speech, to the incidents important for his subsequent narrative. The things which he gives Moses to say, in their selection, combination and particular formulation /2/, are clearly derived from such older accounts. It is usually assumed that he followed the "Hexateuchal" source E here. This is possible /3/, but it will be shown that some of the arguments put forward for the connection of this section with E are not compelling, that Dtr. has at all times related the incidents which he selects from his own point of view and thus somewhat independently of his source or sources, and that in several places he obviously used sources which are no longer extant. This means that we cannot now give a definite specification of the source or sources used by Dtr. for the introductory speech by Moses but can only state in general terms the places where

26

Dtr. is following older accounts.

Thus at the very beginning of the introduction to Moses' speech (Deut. 1:1-5) /4/, we find that Dtr. has used a source no longer extant for the setting of the speech. Although later on he himself sets the speech and Moses' subsequent death (Deut. 3:29; 34:6) at the "valley opposite Beth-Peor" /5/, in Deut. 1:1ff. he uses some place names found nowhere else to give what he himself clearly regards as a precise indication of the place which he has in mind, but these names in fact indicate somewhere quite different /6/. Here we have the fragment of a lost account which presumably makes this the setting for Moses' farewell to the Israelite tribes and which prompted Dtr. to adopt the description of this place in this introduction to Moses' great speech.

After Dtr. has established the historical time /7/ and place in this way, he begins the actual speech with a reminder that God has commanded the Israelites to leave Horeb (Deut. 1:6-8) /8/. Here and subsequently he calls God's mountain not Sinai /9/ as is normal elsewhere in the Old Testament, but Horeb. In this he is following the Deuteronomic law - the name Horeb occurs in the law (Deut. 18:16) albeit as part of a later addition by a secondary hand, and also several times in the later additions of the connecting passages (Deut. 5:2; 9:8; 28:69). Contrary to the common assumption, use of this name is not prompted by the "Hexateuchal" source E; for the only instances of this name in the "Hexateuch", in three passages of Exodus attributed to E, are certainly a later addition /10/. Presumably, then, where "Horeb" occurs in the Deuteronomic law and Dtr., it was taken from a lost source /11/. Similarly, it is hard to believe that Dtr. was drawing on the "Hexateuch" source E when he called the pre-Israelite occupants of arable Palestine "Amorites", even though E almost certainly does use the name in this sense. We should disregard the name where it occurs in the stereotyped lists of nations /12/ and ignore the references to "Amorite" kings of Transjordan and their kingdoms, whether the fault lies in the source or the transmission /13/. This leaves only two instances in which E indisputably used "Amorite" in a general sense: Gen. 15:16 and 48:22. Admittedly, when Dtr. calls the promised land "the hill country of the Amorites" (Deut. 1:7,19,20), alluding to its mountainous terrain, he means the whole of arable Palestine, not just the mountainous parts initially taken over by the Israelites. And in Deut. 1:44 he is clearly not following E's general use of the name but rather the passages in the occupation tradition which he himself adapted, in particular the "kings of the Amorites who lived in the hill-country" in the old account of Jos. 10:6, perhaps also the reference provided by a "compiler" /14/, in Jos. 5:1, to the "kings of the Amorites that were beyond the Jordan", who, unlike the kings of the Canaanites that were by the sea, are to be sought in the inland mountain region (cf. too, Jos. 10:5). Similarly Dtr. draws on the tradition of the occupation of the land in Deut. 1:7 where his enumeration of the different areas of the territory which is to be occupied is evidently based upon the "compiler's" words in Jos. 9:1; 11:16 /15/. Lastly, in extending the promised land as far as the Euphrates, he may be influenced by 1 Kings 5:1 /16/, even if the wording here, with the reference to Lebanon, may seem characteristic of Dtr. /17/. Verse 8ab[a] states briefly the promise of the land and the command to take possession of it /18/.

We have already said that Moses' instructions about the organisation of the Israelite people (Deut. 1:9-18) are mentioned for their relevance to the later activities and battles. These instructions have their prototype in Ex. 18:13ff. and Num. 11:11ff. but Dtr. expresses them in his own way and so arranges them after an explanatory introduction (vv.9-12), we have a report on the installation of military "commanders" and "officers" (vv.13-15), then the indication of the function of the "judges" (vv.16-17) and then a short and allusive reference to the orders Moses gave for the imminent wanderings in the wilderness /19/. We need not go into further detail in this context.

Dtr. tells the story of the spies (Deut. 1:19-46) /20/ in considerable detail within the speech by Moses because, first, it anticipates the theme of occupation which he proposes to treat later in detail; secondly, it helps to explain why the wanderings in the wilderness lasted 40 years and hence to justify Dtr.'s chronology; and thirdly, it provides a motivation for Caleb's special role in the conquest (Jos. 14:6-14). Generally speaking, the material in this section follows a version of the tradition which is also known to us from the various stages of the tradition of Num. 13-14, but we cannot prove that it was derived from any one of these stages /21/. In any case, Dtr. has clearly put this whole section in his own words /22/ and is responsible for the nuances of meaning in the story. We see this right from the beginning where Moses' words of encouragement to the people, reminding them that God has promised them the "hill country of the Amorites" /23/ which is immediately before them, at once meets with mistrust - contrary to the account in Num. 13:1ff. - the people themselves demand a reconnaissance of the land and then at once place an unfavourable construction /24/ on the spies" favourable report. For the first time Dtr. hints at the theme which later takes so many forms in his work - the disobedience and malevolence of the people towards God - which makes them refuse to respond to Moses' entreaty (in Num. 14 Joshua and Caleb attempt this) and finally, as the tradition has it, earns a fitting punishment from God. Caleb's exemption from the punishment pronounced upon all the adult men /25/ belongs to the earliest stratum of the Calebite tradition; and it was necessary in this context to prepare us for Jos. 14:6-14, but it seems inadequately motivated in Deut. 1. We must read between the lines here what Dtr. says explicitly in Jos. 14:8 - that Caleb, unlike his eleven companions, did not succumb to the people's poor morale. But this omission in Deut. 1 can probably be explained by the fact that Dtr. was reproducing a widely familiar story, the outlines of which were common knowledge, and that he was, therefore, occasionally careless in providing a motivation for the details of the tradition.

In the first part of the second chapter, which treats the journeying through the territories of the peoples of Transjordan (Deut. 2:1-25), we are at once struck by Dtr.'s interest in describing a clear and reasonable course of events, here in the form of straightforward information about the route taken by the Israelite tribes, which we do not find in Numbers as we know it. On their way to the "hill country of the Amorites", after they leave Horeb (Deut. 1:6) the tribes reach first the oasis of Kadesh /26/ (1:19), try in vain to advance to the "hill country of the Amorites" only to be sent back to the wilderness and this time in the direction of the "sea of reeds", which means the Gulf of Aqaba, el-ᶜAqaba (1:40). After a long stay in Kadesh (1:46), according to 2:14 two years, they journey towards the Reed Sea and first try to go around Mt Seir, occupied by the Edomites, by going east (2:1), until finally God commands them to change direction and makes the tribes go north through Edomite territory (2:4ff.) /27/ and "away from the Arabah road from Elath and Ezion-geber" (2:8) /28/, by which Dtr. probably means the road through the Wadi el-Jitm and then through the plain el-Ḥesma. According to 2:8b they did not go by the south-north road which would have led right through the area of Moabite settlement; instead they went in the direction of the "wilderness of Moab" /29/, which must mean the desert east of the arable region of Moab. They came first to the brook Zered (2:13), which must mean the upper Wadi el-Hesa, the southern boundary of Moab /30/ (so in the mosaic map of Madeba) and then to the valley of the Arnon (2:24) which bounds the Moabite region on the north, that is on the upper reaches of the Sel el-Mujjib, and from here they finally achieved an entry into the land of Palestine which they were to conquer and occupy /31/.

Apart from this striking interest in itinerary, Dtr.'s only concern in this passage is to remind us that the Israelites were not allowed to touch the Edomite and Moabite territory because this was not the promised land. Furthermore Dtr. differs sharply from Num. 20:14-21 in making the Edomites tacitly permit the Israelite tribes to pass through their land - this is not made explicit but implied beyond a doubt by the sequence of events. Contrary to the view of Steuernagel (ad loc.) this should not be taken to mean that Dtr. was more favourably disposed to the Edomites than was the account of Num. 20:14-21, and hence that Dtr. must be dated before the fall of Jerusalem, the starting point of anti-Edomite feeling during and after the time of exile - despite the fact that Dtr. could have been prompted to treat the Edomites sympathetically merely from Deut. 23:8a. It is obviously better to connect this with Dtr.'s tendency towards a systematic theological interpretation of history such as we can see clearly in Deut. 2 and 3. There the powers which "come out against" the Israelite tribes are defeated and their territory possessed, and these are the powers who live in the land that is promised to the Israelites and that is therefore occupied by them. The later writer who added Deut. 2:30b /32/ stated accurately what Dtr. wished us to read between the lines: the very peoples and states in arable Palestine who were affected by the promise of land to the Israelite tribes prepared the way for their own destruction by their opposition that was rooted in a divine "hardening". From this Dtr. inferred that if the Edomite land was not part of the promised land (as indeed the course of history was to show), then the Edomites would not have put up any resistance - otherwise their territory would have had to be conquered by force. It is obviously this consideration that lies behind Dtr.'s deviation from Num. 20:14-21 /33/. Furthermore, Dtr.'s account does not allow for even the possibility of conflict between the

Moabites and the Israelites, since the Israelites do not even go through Moabite territory but only through the "wilderness of Moab" /34/. It was a later writer who misunderstood this and on the analogy of v.5 interpolated v.9a^{b}b which is particularly conspicuous for its singular addressee, for v.13 which follows it without a break /35/ goes back to a plural addressee and v.13 is patently the beginning of a divine commandment /36/ and so belongs after v.9a^a. The same later author brought in the Ammonites in vv.18,19, again with an unmotivated use of a singular address, to complete the series of three southern peoples of Transjordan, even though the route determined by Dtr. could not have brought the Israelites into immediate contact with the Ammonites. Very strikingly, after the verses attributable to him in Deut. 2:1-25 - that is, 1-6,8,9a^a, 13-17,24a^a - Dtr. reports nothing between the crossing of the Zered valley and the order to cross the Arnon valley. This supports the view that he is here primarily interested in establishing the itinerary. Only at the beginning of the section on the journey through Edomite territory does he give an example of the Israelites' conduct towards the peoples of southern Transjordan. The reference to the death of the old generation and thus to the end of the wanderings in the desert appropriately follows the report of the crossing of the Zered valley, since the next stage, the crossing of the Arnon valley, was the first step in the occupation of the promised land, which the old generation was not to live to see; the close connection between vv.16,17 and 24a^a makes this quite clear. Meanwhile Dtr. implies in v.15 that he knew traditions of various events that had taken place on the way between the Zered and Arnon valleys which it was not part of his plan to enumerate.

Dtr. divides the section of Moses' speech on the occupation and settlement of Transjordan (Deut. 2:26-3:22) into three parts: (i) the defeat of the two Transjordanian kings Sihon and Og (2:26-3:7), (ii) the allocation of their land to two and a half Israelite tribes (3:8-17), (iii) the commitment of these tribes to take part in the conquest of the land west of the Jordan (3:18-22). Dtr. makes the sections on Sihon and Og as parallel as possible in their structure and wording, and indeed it is he who is responsible for juxtaposing these two kings with one another. King Og of Bashan appears in the Old Testament only in the work of Dtr. and in other later passages dependent on this work /37/, and always as a parallel to king Sihon of Heshbon. Dtr. certainly is relying upon a source known to him but lost to us, the original nature of which cannot be reconstructed. There is, in fact, an older account of Sihon of Heshbon in Num. 21:21-31. Dtr. does not indicate the historical context in which he found the tradition about Og. In 2:26ff. /38/ he relies on Num. 21 and, unquestionably, motivates the battle against Sihon by saying that Sihon, whose land was directly in the path of the Israelites, given their route thus far, decided to resist; but the campaign against Og who lived a long way off (3:1ff.) /39/ is not explained at all, but just described as if parallel to the campaign against Sihon. Dtr. needed to juxtapose Sihon and Og because, in keeping with his concept of the historical process as simple and according to a plan, he saw the occupation of the whole of Transjordan including the north as a self-contained event before the conquest of the promised land. At the beginning of the Sihon story, for the reasons given above, Dtr. emphasises the contrast between his behaviour and that of the Edomites and Moabites (2:26-30a) /40/. After the victory over Sihon at Jahaz (given as the scene of battle as early as Num. 21:23) and similarly, after the victory over Og (3:6f.) the defeated enemy are "put to the ban", though their cattle and possessions are saved for the conquerors (2:32-35) - as is customary in the occupation tradition known to Dtr. (Jos. 8:2,27; 11:14) /41/ - and the whole land is occupied, from the border of the Arnon, which is expressed in a traditional formula /42/, to a vague boundary somewhere in the land of "Gilead" in which Dtr. includes northern el-Belka and all of Ajlun /43/, as we see from 3:12f. The corresponding observation on the extent of Og's kingdom in 3:4,5 names, inter alia, the whole region of Argob which probably was, as in 1 Kings 4:13, the region of the district governor in Ramoth-Gilead, and is probably to be located north-east of Ajlun. In the original text of Dtr. the section on the allocation of the conquered land to some Israelite tribes (3:8-17) was fairly short and merely made a reference to the total extent of the territory in the region in question (3:8) /44/ to tell us that the southern half, broadly corresponding to the former kingdom of Sihon, went jointly to the Reubenites and Gadites (3:12) /45/, and the northern half, the former kingdom of Og /46/, to the half tribe of Manasseh (3:13a). These short notices lent themselves to all manner of later augmentation. Apart from the reference to Hermon's different titles (3:9), the note (connected with 2:10-12,20-23) that Og belonged to the aboriginal population (3:11) /47/, and the information about the original population of Argob (3:13b), we have, in the first instance, supplementary information on the geography of the settlement; in v.10, an additional indication of the total area taken from Jos. 13:9-11; in v.14 (in which "as it is to this day" looks conspicuously out of place /48/), an expansion based on Num. 32:41; in v.15, material from Num. 32:39; and in vv.16-17, an addition based on Jos. 12:2-3. The section on the commitment of the two and a half Transjordanian tribes to help in the conquest (3:18-22), the ending of which (vv.21-22) is a secondary anticipation of 3:28 compiled from stock Deuteronomistic formulae, is repeated in Jos. 1:13-15 with a few variations in wording and arrangement. What Moses tells the Transjordanian tribes here /49/, Joshua later brings home to them, according to Dtr., with explicit reference to the words of Moses, at the moment when this commitment needs to be acted upon.

Moses' reference to his own death and the succession of Joshua (3:23-29) explains why Moses must now present the people with the detailed explanation of the ten commandments proclaimed at Horeb (which God gave him there); that is, the Deuteronomic law (cf. Deut. 5:28 and p.16 above). Moses dies shortly after he has seen God's great deeds begin (v.24); this is accounted for, not by his personal guilt, as in Num. 20:12, but by the guilt of the people seen by Dtr. as a well-established fact /50/ and therefore not specifically explained. Moses as the responsible leader must bear the consequences of this guilt /51/. Moses' petition (v.25) to be allowed to enter Cisjordan, which here, as in Deut. 1:7 includes "the Lebanon", is used merely to lead into God's denial of the petition.

Once this retrospective summary of those events of the Mosaic period important for Dtr.'s history is at an end, and it is time to proclaim the law, the speech develops into a general introduction to the law (Deut. 4:1-40). Since the law as Dtr. knew it already had a long admonitory introduction, this transitional passage was certainly not required by the context and, indeed, it is questionable whether Deut. 4:1-40 is to be attributed to Dtr. or seen as a later addition. The section Deut. 4:1-40 lacks inner unity. It is easy to see that the parts with a singular addressee are by a secondary hand /52/ but even in the remainder, all is not clear /53/. This is especially apparent in vv.10-18. After the reference to the theophany at Horeb (vv.10-12) /54/ we are reminded, on the one hand, in vv.13-14, of the law of the ten commandments written on the two stone tablets /55/, as a covenant ordinance /56/, and of the detailed "teaching" about this law with which Moses was charged; on the other hand, in vv.15-18 we have a statement connected with one of the last words in v.12, saying that one cannot and may not try to portray God in creaturely form. The two continuations of vv.10-12 could not have stood side by side originally, as the gap between v.14 and v.15 shows. Verses 13-14 are usually regarded as later additions and the command not to make graven images seen as the main theme of Deut. 4:1-24, but it is just as plausible that vv.15-18 are perhaps a subsequent explication of the last words of v.12 which are not particularly emphasised but just added, in passing, to the account of the theophany on Sinai. This latter hypothesis is in fact correct, since the explanatory sentence v.22, which is generally and rightly counted as part of the original text, is unrelated to v.18 /57/ but closely linked with v.14 - it explains God's command to Moses to tell the people the "statutes" they should obey in the promised land by saying that Moses is to die before the occupation of the land, but the Israelites are to enter the land /58/. The other elements of the original text in this chapter - vv.1-2,5-8,10-14,22-23a,25-28 /59/ - fit the context of Dtr.'s history perfectly and so confirm the conclusion indicated by the position of the chapter, namely that here Dtr. inserted an interlude, on the lines of the great introductory speech which follows, between the recollection of events and the narration of the law as he knew it. Beginning with the solemn formulaic singular sm^c ("hear"), Dtr. has Moses instruct the Israelite tribes about the importance of the definitive and immutable law which he is about to teach them (vv.1,2,5) /60/, and explain to them that in possessing the law they have a special advantage over other peoples (vv.6-8). Moses takes the opportunity to remind them of the fundamental events of the theophany in Horeb and the proclamation of the decalogue (vv.10-14); here Dtr. briefly and skilfully incorporates a short account of the events at Horeb. Moses then reminds them of the basis of the covenant concluded there (vv.22-23a) and finishes by drawing the tribes' attention, in solemn terms, to the grave consequences of disregarding God's commandments (vv.25-28); here Dtr. puts into Moses' mouth the lessons learned from subsequent history with which he himself is familiar. Then the Deuteronomic law is given in its entirety.

Afterwards, in Deut. 31, Dtr. continues with the narrative which broke off in Deut. 1:5 when it was interrupted by the great speech of Moses, the first part of which he wrote himself and the second part of which is made up of the Deuteronomic law. He uses this narrative to report the last instructions and death of Moses. Moses, following God's instructions in Deut. 3:28, designates Joshua as his successor (Deut. 31:1-2,7-8) /61/. Furthermore, Dtr. has Moses write down the law (v.9a[a]) /62/ and, no doubt on the basis of an actual practice known to him from history, makes him prescribe that the law should be read out every seventh year at the autumn festival (vv.10,11a[b]b, 12b-13 /63/). Even though this last prescription is expressed in exclusively Deuteronomistic language, it seems not to have come into this section until later (possibly due to Dtr. himself), as vv.24-26 is directly linked to v.9a[a]. Here Moses has the Levites place the law written down by him beside the ark of the covenant - this assumes that the ark already had a fixed location - since the Mosaic law takes second place to the decalogue given at Horeb but is closely linked to it as its exposition /64/. Immediately after this Dtr. reports Moses' death - fragments of the report survive in Deut. 34:1 (in particular r'š hpsgh), 4 (cf. 3:27), 5-6 (cf. 3:29). Before this and after the law has been deposited in its place (Deut. 32:46-47), we have the last words of Moses, which were inserted at a later stage; the song of Moses (Deut. 32:1-43) and the passages in Deuteronomistic language immediately before and after it (Deut. 31:27b-30; 32:44-45) came into Dtr.'s history even later /65/. At this stage the attempt began to harmonise the narrative with that of the Pentateuch: before Moses' last speech the story of Joshua's consecration in Deut. 31:14,15,23 was inserted /66/, but the account of Moses' death is set down alongside the Pentateuchal version (Deut. 32:48-52; 34:*1-12) which is interwoven with the parts of Dtr.'s narrative mentioned above. Finally the introduction to the song of Moses (Deut. 31:16-22), inserted rather clumsily in the middle of the self-contained passage Deut. 31:14,15,23, was added much later, as was the "blessing of Moses" (Deut. 33:1-29), which is not related to anything that comes before or after it.

The presence of <u>narrative</u> elements of Dtr.'s history in Deut. 31-34 which have nothing to do with the framework of the Deuteronomic law but are related to Deut. 1-4 in their subject matter confirms our thesis that Dtr.'s history is designed as a large-scale <u>narrative</u>.

Chapter Six
THE OCCUPATION OF THE LAND WEST OF THE JORDAN

According to the historical outline of Dtr., which was already traditional when the author received it, the next event to be dealt with was the occupation of Palestine west of the Jordan after the death of Moses. For this Dtr. had access to a self-contained and detailed account, already existing in a fixed literary form. This account was composed long before Dtr.; a series of separate aetiological stories relevant to the Israelites" successful incursion /1/ was combined into a well-rounded whole with a few heroic legends /2/. Dtr. obviously took the whole of this over and altered it only by adding an introduction and epilogue and some supplementary material /3/.

The introduction is in Jos. 1. We have no reason to suppose that there are pre-Deuteronomistic elements in this chapter with its thoroughly Deuteronomistic language - although this is a long-standing hypothesis of literary criticism. If we take Dtr.'s approach into account, all the details are easily explained. In a short address to Joshua, Yahweh says that the imminent task is to conquer the promised land west of the Jordan; the extent of this land is briefly indicated in vv.1-4, based on Deut. 1:7; then addressing Joshua individually, in the singular, he repeats the encouraging words of Deut. 31:7-8 at this crucial moment, with some changes in the order (vv.5-6) /4/. Then Joshua repeats to the two and a half tribes who have already taken possession of Transjordan (Deut. 3:12-13a) Moses' injunction that they should take part in the campaign on the other side of the river, changing the word order only slightly and referring explicitly to Deut. 3:18-20; this injunction now (vv.10-11) has practical importance and is acknowledged by the two and a half tribes (vv.16-18) /5/. After these introductory sections in which Dtr. establishes the context, and which are determined by his preconceptions, Jos. 2:1 begins the traditional account of the occupation; here Dtr. has added, in the first instance, only a few remarks which he thinks important. For example, in Jos. 2:10b he brings in a reference to the defeat of two Transjordanian "Amorite kings" /6/; admittedly this is practically indispensable, given the narrative up to this point. In Jos. 3:4 the holy ark played a central role, even in the older accounts; here Dtr. inserts some verses emphasising the leading role of this sacred object which he too thinks very important (3:2,3,4b,6,8) /7/. Furthermore, this emphasis runs consistently through the whole passage; the word "priests" is set beside the traditional title "bearers of the ark" (3:13,14,15,17; 4:3,9,10,18) and this expresses his feeling that the ark must of necessity receive sacred treatment /8/. Besides, in treating the first major action to take place under Joshua he lays great stress on an idea which had significance for him (3:7; 4:14; 4:24): Joshua like Moses is assured of divine help (cf. Deut. 31:8; Jos. 1:5[17]). Dtr. repeats that the Transjordanian tribes actually helped the others (4:12). As for the additions to the circumcision scene (Jos. 5:2-9), vv. 4, 6 and 7 must be attributed to Dtr. because of their language - in them the existence of a circumcision commandment which does not in fact occur in the Deutero-nomic law is assumed, and as an explanation of Jos. 5:2,3(5),8,9, the death of the older generation (for the reasons given in Deut. 1:34,35,39a^{b}b) during the 40-year (Deut.1:3) wandering in the wilderness (Deut. 2:14-16) is mentioned /9/. In Jos. 6, a chapter which does not lend itself readily to literary analysis, the introduction of the priests may be traced back to Dtr., and the ark, certainly not originally part of this story, would have been brought in even before Dtr. because of its function in Jos. 3:4 (v.7b + 9b,11,13b). At this point Dtr. brought the priests in as bearers of the ark (v.6a) but, more particularly, as the persons in charge of the trumpet-blowing mentioned as part of the traditional account in v.5a and understood by Dtr. as a religious ritual (vv.4a^{a}b,6b,8,9a,12b,13a,16a^b) - this is consistent with his procedure in Jos. 3:4 and his general attitude to matters of cult. Finally, Dtr. understandably made a point of hinting at the later fate of the city of Jericho; this is based on information from official sources which he gives in 1 Kings 16:34. Dtr. seems not to have touched the Ai story (Jos. 7-8), except that at the beginning of the divine speech in 8:1a we see a small addition of his, while 8:1b-2a, which is already important in the old accounts of the occupation, is later used for the addition Deut. 3:2 (Num. 21:34).

After the Ai story Dtr. inserts a whole passage of his own composition, Jos. 8:30-35. This is all in Deuteronomistic language and can be sufficiently accounted for by Dtr.'s own assumptions; we have no reason whatsoever to assume an earlier source /10/. Here Dtr. reports the execution of Moses' instructions (Deut. 27:2ff.) which he had found in the framework

passages of the Deuteronomic law. Jos. 8:30-35 is derived from
Deut. 27:2ff., not the other way round /11/. This is so because
Jos. 8:31a[b]b takes over the account in Deut. 27:5-7a[a],
which is rather complicated, possibly because of the complex
literary history of this passage, and summarises it in one clear,
simple sentence without changing the expression very much.
Similarly in Jos. 8:34-35, which is directly connected with what
goes before, Dtr. alludes explicitly to Deut. 31:11b (Jos.
8:35b[a]) in reporting the fulfilment of the order given in Deut.
31:*10-13. Dtr., then, has concluded that the instructions which
he found in Deut. 27:2ff. were carried out by Joshua as soon as
possible and that this was made possible once the conquest of
Ai had opened the way for the Israelites to the mountain area
of Ephraim /12/. To this Dtr. adds only the reference to the
presence of the ark at the sacred ritual - he saw this ritual as
the obvious sequel to previous events (Jos. 3; 4:6), but he would
think special mention of it appropriate to justify the building of
the altar at Shechem. Thus in Jos. 8:30-35 Dtr. has inferred a
historical event, for which he had no source, from Deut. 27:2ff.
(and Deut. 31:10ff.) and inserted it at what he considered to be
the appropriate place in the traditional historical sequence.

After this he follows the old account of the occupation again
except that in Jos. 9:9b[b]-10 he thinks it necessary because of
his own preconceptions to refer not only to the exodus from
Egypt but in particular to the defeat of the two Transjordanian
"Amorite" kings, and in Jos. 9:27b[b] he brings in the stereotyped Deuteronomic formula for the site of the legitimate
sanctuary; in Jos. 10:25 he embellishes the old story in typical
Deuteronomistic language, and in Jos. 11:15,20b at the end of
the process of occupation he emphasises how scrupulously
Joshua carried out God's orders to Moses (cf. 8:31,35), meaning
here the command to destroy the enemy totally (Deut.
20:16-18). The old story of the occupation was clearly rounded
off with a summary composed by the "compiler" (Jos. 11:16-20a)
but Dtr. adds an observation of his own (Jos. 11:20b) and goes on
to attach another passage of his own devising. Note that Jos.
14:6a[b]b-15a in its present setting is not related to the
introduction 14:6a[a] and does not fit the context if read with
the final sentence (Jos. 14:15b); its original place was before
Jos. 11:23b as is shown by the fact that Jos. 14:15b is the same
as Jos. 11:23b /13/. There we see that after Dtr. inserted the
occupation tradition, he first took, from a source unknown to
us, the statement (vv.21-22) that the Anakim were destroyed;

this is part of the "conquest" theme and is necessary to prepare us for subsequent events. Then in v.23a^a he briefly establishes that the whole land had now been conquered. In v.23a^b he moves on to the theme of "the distribution of the land"; he states in very cursory and general terms that the land was distributed among the Israelite tribes in order then, in relation to this theme, to tell a particular story of the giving of the territory of the Anakim at Hebron to Caleb (14:6a^{b}b-15a), indicating that by this means the land came to have peace (11:23b=14:15b). The Caleb story he clearly composed himself, basing it on traditional material /14/, just as he composed the spy story in Deut. 1:19-46 which anticipates the Caleb story. Why does he treat this apparently minor episode in such detail after referring to the division of the land in such general terms in 11:23a^b? The explanation must be as follows. He wanted to use for the occupation theme all the material he knew: he knew the relevant stories of the spies and of Caleb from the "Hexateuchal" sources, but in order to use these stories, of which he may have known variant forms, he had to detach them from their traditional contexts; so he did not give the traditional version but modified it somewhat to serve his purposes. As a whole, Jos. 14:6a^{b}b-15a reads as though Dtr. expanded a story based on a promise to Caleb contained in the spy story, such a promise as actually exists in Num. 14:24.

To supplement the occupation story Dtr. characteristically enumerates the lands conquered and the enemy kings defeated by the Israelite tribes (Jos. 12). In keeping with Dtr.'s approach thus far, the enumeration falls into two parallel sections, the Cisjordanian and the Transjordanian. The Transjordanian section briefly repeats what is said in Deut. 3:8,12,13a and has been subsequently extended, particularly with reference to Jos. 13 /15/. For the Cisjordanian section, Dtr. took the delineation of the whole area (v.7a^b) from the "compiler's" final note in Jos. 11:17 and in order to enumerate the territories (v.8a) combined the "compiler's" statements in Jos. 10:40 and 11:16 /16/. Over and above this, he took from the old tradition the names of defeated Canaanite cities (vv.9-13a) /17/ and immediately afterwards in vv.13b-24a added to these from a source now lost, giving the cities of Canaan in geographical order.

In Jos. 23 Dtr. gives the long speech by Joshua which finishes off the whole occupation story. Dtr.'s account is constructed in such a way that this speech marks the end of an historical epoch and, looking back to the great events now at an end, goes on to warn the people against the gods and cults of the land that has now been taken for a possession, and culminates in a threat of retribution. It cannot be accidental that this threat resembles in meaning and wording the threat at the end of that part of Moses' great speech composed by Dtr. (Deut. 4:25-28, esp. v.26).

The long section on the settlement of the individual tribes (Jos. 13-22) is not originally part of Dtr.'s work, as we see from the fact that the introduction in 13:1a anticipates 23:1b word for word and also from the fact that Dtr. has already (Jos. 11:23a^b) mentioned the distribution of the conquered area among the tribes - briefly, to be sure, but in terms suggesting that he has finished with the topic. However, the language and attitude of this section are very akin to Dtr. One must assume that it was interpolated soon after the completion of Dtr.'s work, in keeping with his approach and in his spirit. In particular the closing section, Jos. 21:43-22:6 /18/, is so close to Dtr. in style that one could attribute it to Dtr. himself, except that, like the rest of the chapter, it comes after Jos. 11:23a^b, which is too late, and 21:44-45 inappropriately anticipates sentences from Joshua's last speech (Jos. 23:9b,14b). Thus we conclude that a later writer augmented Dtr.'s version at this point with very valuable historical material, transforming a description based on two different documents of the possessions of the twelve Israelite tribes after the conquest into a narrative of the distribution of the land to the tribes at the time of the conquest and integrating this into Dtr.'s account after Jos. 12 /19/. This transformation and integration can be observed particularly in the following instances. In keeping with the pattern of Dtr.'s history, the sections on the two and a half Transjordanian tribes had to be anticipated and brought into the present context in the form of a passage which delays the progress of the narrative (Jos. 13). The old heading which was meant to cover the whole section /20/ was left unchanged in Jos. 14:1a; then vv.2b^b-3a /21/ was added to make it refer specifically to the other nine and a half tribes. Judah and Joseph (Manasseh and Ephraim) were put first because they were apparently the first to take the initiative to settle their future homeland; this the later author apparently took from the narrative sources at his disposal. In any case, Jos. 14:6a^a begins a separate story about Judah which is not properly related to the story of Caleb which follows it (vv.6a^{b}b-15). Possibly, since the Caleb story belongs to the theme of the division of the land, the later author took it out of Dtr.'s version after Jos. 11:23a[b] and inserted it in Jos. 14 under the heading "Judah" - since he was obliged to keep the twelve tribes in his arrangement of the material /22/. Joseph was probably put at the beginning because the later author concluded from Jos. 17:14-18 that this tribe too took the initiative in the occupation. As for the seven remaining tribes, the later author has inserted in Jos. 18:*1-10 the act of the casting of the lot for the seven parcels of land and expresses this in the formulation of the headings found in 18:11; 19:1,10,17,24,32,40. Finally the later author was relying on a plan of unknown origin for a new order after the restitution of Israel /23/ when he added the passage on the cities of asylum (Jos. 20) which originally was probably very short and not expanded until later. At the end of the whole section the later author puts the concluding passage Jos. 21:43-45 and reports that the two and a half Transjordanian tribes were authorised to return home (Jos. 22:1-6). This last piece of information would have been superfluous for Dtr. since Jos. 11:23a[b] implies that the tribes dispersed into the territories allocated to each, whereas the later author thinks (18:*1-10) that apart from Judah and Joseph (cf. 18:5) the tribes were still together on the final occasion of casting the lot, that they were in Gilgal (cf. 14:6a[a] and the language of 18:5) /24/ and that the Transjordanian tribes had been promised their land by Moses but not yet taken possession of it. Like Dtr. the later author worked deliberately and according to plan.

Chapter Seven
THE PERIOD OF THE "JUDGES"

Immediately after Jos. 23, in Judg. 2:6ff., Dtr. introduces a new period in the history of Israel, the time of the "judges". He sees this period as continuing until 1 Sam. 12, as appears from the fact that Samuel's great speech in 1 Sam. 12 corresponds to Joshua's last speech in Jos. 23. This speech culminates in a threat of retribution similar to that in the speech by Joshua and in the part of Moses' great speech written by Dtr. (Deut. 1:6-4:28). In keeping with this division, Dtr. begins the monarchic period with the formulaic introduction to his account of Saul in 1 Sam. 13:1. The period of the individual heroes and "minor judges" (Judg. 2:6-12:15) and the period of the prophet Samuel come from two different traditions. The background of the second period is the Philistine oppression which begins in Judg. 13:1, and this period culminates in the rise of the monarchy. But to simplify the division of the history into periods Dtr. attributed everything between the completion of the occupation and the beginning of the reign of the first king to the period of the "judges" and, quite consistently, included Samuel's career in this latter period.

For his account of the "judges" period up to Samuel, Dtr. used and combined two basic traditions. The first was a series of stories about various tribal heroes and their victories, which came from different sources /1/ but were probably collected together before Dtr. They still lacked thematic unity and so Dtr. had to supply them with connecting material /2/. The second was a list of "judges" (whom we call "minor judges") with short accounts of their birthplaces, the periods of their office and places of burial and sometimes the odd detail about their lives. This list is obviously based on old records of an office held by one incumbent after another without interruption. The office, like the reigns of kings later on, was probably used for chronological purposes - hence the exact figures given for the duration of each term of office - and it was responsible for the preservation of justice. A. Alt adduces the illuminating parallel of the Icelandic "proclaimers of the law" /3/. We shall immediately see that in Dtr.'s conception of the "judges" it was essential that he should establish a connection between the

42

tales of heroes and the "judge" list /4/. Why did he connect them? He did so not simply because both traditions had to do with the time between the occupation and the rise of the monarchy, but, more particularly, because they intersect at one specific point, namely in the figure of Jephthah. Undoubtedly Dtr. came across this character in a story of a tribal hero, one of a series of such stories. On the other hand, he certainly found him also in the list of the "(minor) judges" and from this list took the information given in Judg. 12:7. It is very conspicuous that Dtr. finishes his account of Jephthah not as he usually does, by saying that there were 40 years of "rest" after the victory of the hero concerned, but with details which follow the system used in the list of "(minor) judges": a statement concerning his six-year period of office /5/, then the report of his death and place of burial /6/. To this Dtr. attaches statements about three other "judges" who succeeded one another without a break and came immediately after Jephthah. Given Jephthah's presence in both traditions /7/, it is easy to account for the arrangement of material in Judges. The "minor judges" come immediately before and after the Jephthah story: Judg. 10-12 is obviously based on the series of minor judges as Dtr. knew it - Tola, Jair, Jephthah, Ibzan, Elon, Abdon - but the account of Jephthah has been excessively swollen by the heroic material already extant and so we lose the sense of a cohesive series of "(minor) judges". At this point the great heroic narratives in Judges loom so large that the chapters on the "(minor) judges" look like two interruptions located here for no apparent reason /8/.

Now it was this conjunction of the two traditions in the figure of Jephthah which caused Dtr. to call the heroes of the great legends "judges" as well. This was certainly not their original title since, generally speaking, neither the tradition nor Dtr. shows them acting in a judicial capacity /9/, but rather as charismatic military leaders. O. Grether has conclusively proved /10/ that there is no demonstrable or even plausible meaning for the word "judge" which could apply to these heroes as we know them. Instead, seeing that the military hero Jephthah appears in the "judge" list, Dtr. has assumed that the other legendary heroes played an analogous role as "judges", or possibly vice versa: since the "judge" Jephthah appears also as a military hero, Dtr. may have thought that the charismatic leadership of the tribes in war was an important part of the authority or duty of the judge. In any case he refers to the

43

great heroes as "judges" particularly in the general introduction
to the "judges" period in Judg. 2:16,18 /11/ where the narrative
of the deeds of the heroes is of such paramount importance to
him that he gives no consideration to the "(minor) judges" when
introducing them, even though the title originates with them.

Dtr. has also extended the significance of the "(minor)
judges" for the whole of Israel to apply to the heroes - not that
in the traditional heroic stories the importance of the narrated
events for Israel as a whole was completely lacking. The name
Israel occurs here repeatedly /12/; and we need not suppose that
Dtr. was the first to introduce it /13/. Obviously the old heroic
stories had already been collected to illustrate Israel's disputes
with her hostile neighbours in the period after the conquest,
disputes which took the form of isolated battles between
individual tribes or groups of tribes and their foreign
neighbours. Dtr. ignored this detail and gave each hero credit
for liberating the whole of Israel from foreign rule, each
liberation being followed by 40 years of peace for all Israel. So
he represents the heroes as holders of one and the same office,
with intervals between one hero and the next; here his model
was clearly the tradition of the "(minor) judges" as holders of a
fixed office. Therefore he has taken the formal framework of
the "judges" period from the tradition of the "(minor) judges"
and filled in this framework principally with the traditional
heroic narrative cycle.

In his treatment of the "judges" period, Dtr. was particularly
concerned to portray the people's repeated apostasy. The divine
help apparent in the victories remains in evidence only until
those who witnessed it have died (in the 40-year periods of
"rest" /14/). Then the apostasy sets in again and it is worse each
time; Dtr. probably means by wyspw, which introduces most of
the sections (Judg. 3:12; 4:1; 10:6; 13:1), "(their evildoing)
became worse still", since he has stated in the introduction that
each successive generation "behaved worse than their fathers"
(2:19).

There is little more to be said of the first part of Dtr.'s
account of the "judges" period. The source of the Othniel story
(Judg. 3:7-11) remains an unsolved mystery. As a whole, it is
composed by Dtr. Apart from the reference to the death of
Othniel (v.11b), the statement, of uncertain origin, that "the
spirit of Yahweh came upon him and he judged Israel"
(v.10a[a]) /15/ is a noteworthy departure from the usual framework.

In the Ehud story (Judg. 3:12-30), vv.12-15a and v.30b are the framework composed by Dtr. The brief reference to Shamgar (Judg. 3:31) attached to this was already part of Dtr.'s account. Dtr. had it in mind when he calculated the time of "rest" in v.30b at twice forty years /16/. Perhaps Dtr. took this reference from the collection of heroic stories which he used.

Dtr. shaped the framework of the Deborah-Barak story (Judg. 4:1-5:31) in 4:1a,2,3a /17/ and 5:31b and probably added, on the basis of 4:5, the awkwardly integrated remark concerning Deborah's "judging" (4:4b). The secondary connection between Sisera and Jabin king of Hazor had already been made in Dtr.'s source (cf. 4:7,17,23,24). But Dtr. took it over without noticing that the old account of the occupation which he himself had previously adapted had noted that this Jabin had been killed in the time of Joshua (Jos. 11:10) and, since the city of Hazor had been destroyed at that time (Jos. 11:11b,13b), Dtr. could not have assumed that there was a later king of the same name who ruled the same city without contradicting himself. Such inconsistencies are nothing out of the ordinary in historical works which have absorbed various old sources.

The long Gideon story (Judg. 6:1-8:32) had already been compiled in the old tradition out of various different elements; to it Dtr. provides a relatively detailed introduction. He merely follows his usual practice by prefixing to the old account of the Midianite oppression (6:2-6a) a statement that the apostasy brought about this external affliction (6:1); but he also introduces an unnamed prophet who says that the incongruity between God's saving activities and the people's disobedience has grown greater and greater (6:6b-10) /18/. The prophet provides a reflection upon the situation such as Dtr. on occasion likes to put into his characters' mouths. That in this situation God is nevertheless ready to help is implied in the old Gideon story which follows immediately. Dtr.'s epilogue to the Gideon story goes well beyond the framework of the usual short formulaic conclusion because it has, at the same time, to serve as an introduction to the Abimelech story (Judg. 9:1-57). We cannot doubt that this passage, too, derives from Dtr. In the first place, the first section on the "(minor) judges" (Judg. 10:1) links up explicitly with the Abimelech story /19/. In the second place, it was Dtr. and not a later author who initially tailored the end of the Gideon story to the needs of the Abimelech story. This is shown not only by the clearly Deuteronomistic style of Judg. 8:33-35 but also in the extension of the formulaic ending (v.28) to state explicitly that Gideon lived through the whole 40 years of "rest", whereas this was not said of the earlier heroes. This extension also has to do with the line of thought which prompted Dtr. to link the Gideon and Abimelech stories /20/. The story of Gideon's golden ephod (vv.24-27a) was clearly conceived in the old account as an innocent piece of local history, but in v.27b Dtr. indicates that Gideon thereby encouraged the "Israelites" to practise an idolatrous cult and so was himself to blame for the disaster which struck his family immediately after his death. To be sure, he himself did not take part in this cult /21/ and, as a saviour appointed by God, prevented the worst from happening and thus made possible the 40 years' period of "rest" which continued as long as he was alive. Dtr. describes his death in uncharacteristic detail (v.32) because immediately thereafter the restraints vanished and the "Israelites" succumbed to unmitigated idolatry (vv.33,34) and thus brought upon Gideon's family (v.35) the disaster for which Gideon was essentially to blame; this Dtr. shows in the story of Abimelech which follows, according to the traditional sequence /22/.

Dtr. wrote an even more detailed introduction to the Jephthah story (Judg. 10:6-12:6), prefixing to the old beginning of the story (10:17) a long explanatory passage (10:6-16) which is clearly meant to accentuate what was said in previous introductions including that to the Gideon story. For example, at the beginning v.6 notes that the Israelites now took up the worship not just of local gods but of the gods of all the neighbouring peoples; this is why the Ammonite /23/ oppression which begins at this point is so heavy, in that it not only "crushed" /24/ the adjacent Transjordanian settlement, the country of the two defeated "Amorite" kings /25/, but also reached west of the Jordan (vv.8,9). And although the Israelites recognise that they are now more guilty than ever and confess their sins (v.10) as well as crying for help (v.10), Yahweh begins by reminding them of their ingratitude (vv.11-13a) /26/ and refusing to help (vv.13b,14). Only after they have again entreated him urgently (v.15) and have decisively rejected the alien gods whom they worshipped (v.16a) will God intervene. This whole section gives clear evidence of Dtr.'s intention to show how the people's conduct towards God constantly deteriorated throughout the period of the "judges"; and so at this point the last historical example of the pattern set out in Judg. 2:11ff. virtually culminates in a complete severance of relations between the people and their God. After the traditional Jephthah story /27/ and the rest of the "judges" list Dtr. passes to the Philistine oppression and the career of Samuel, which lead directly up to the rise of the monarchy, and thus this theme of deterioration is not further continued.

In this, the second part of the "judges" period, Dtr.'s main source was the beginning of the old Saul-David tradition. Dtr. uses this tradition, made up of diverse elements /28/, to describe the rest of the "judges" period, until he reports the accession of Saul (1 Sam. 11:15). At exactly this point Dtr. intended the "judges" period to end and the "kings" period to begin. For the end of the "judges" period, then, he had to use the first part of the "ark narrative" (1 Sam 4:1b-7:1) and the related tradition of Saul's accession (1 Sam. 9:1-10:16 and 10:27b-11:15), from that tradition complex. On the basis of the "ark narrative" the domination by the Philistines – the historical background for the events portrayed – was, as far as he was concerned, to be depicted analogously with the previous cases of foreign domination throughout the period of the "judges" (Judg. 13:1) /29/. Dtr. thought that the rise of the monarchy was of fundamental importance; with hindsight afforded by the situation in his own time, he inevitably concluded that the monarchy had led the Israelite nation to destruction – a theme that he developed in his treatment of the details of his history. In the "judges" period the continual apostasies of the Israelites brought them near the abyss (cf. Judg. 10:6-16); similarly Dtr. now held the monarchy responsible and judged that it was Israel's kings who, not immediately but finally, had laid it low. This explains why, in treating this event which he thought so important, Dtr. abandoned his normal practice of basically letting the old accounts speak for themselves and setting forth his own theological interpretation of history only in the introductions and conclusions. Here instead he composes the narrative himself and develops it at length; his narratives are meant not to correct the old account but to fill it out with the elements he thought important.

Wellhausen /30/ was certainly right to claim that the passages 1 Sam. 7:2-8:22, 10:17-27a, and 12:1-25, which have a common theme, are to be ascribed to Dtr. on the ground of their language and their subject matter; and he rightly points out that they presuppose the existence of the older tradition in 1 Sam. 9-11 and are composed in relation to this. Since the present tendency is to see these passages as the bare bones of a self-contained pre-Deuteronomistic narrative /31/, we must examine this question briefly and can take the opportunity to clarify the assumptions and intentions of Dtr. in these passages.

After bringing in the first part of the "ark narrative" according to the text of the old tradition /32/ and thereby giving a vivid illustration of the period of Philistine rule, Dtr. introduces Samuel as a "judge" in the sense of the book of Judges (1 Sam. 7:2-17). Whether or not he knew an account of Samuel engaging in judicial activity - which, on the strength of 1 Sam. 7:16,17 he could well have done - his own conception of the "judges" period would have led him to make "judges" of all persons of significance for the whole of Israel during the period between the occupation and the monarchy, including Samuel; so, for Samuel, like the others, he emphasises and repeats the general statement, "he judged Israel" /33/. But in Dtr.'s view, the major "judges" had to save their country, and from this he inferred that the end of the Philistine oppression must be attributed to a decisive victory by Samuel; indeed, that such oppression existed in his time was already attested in the tradition. Moreover, his general dislike of the monarchy would inevitably prompt him to deny that the defeat of the Philistines (1 Sam. 13:2ff.) by Saul, the first king, which is known from the old tradition and admittedly did take place very shortly before Saul's crushing defeat by the Philistines (1 Sam. 31), was responsible for putting a final end to Philistine rule (cf. Judg. 13:1) and for the avenging of injuries (1 Sam. 4), and he would, therefore, see Saul's Philistine wars as a mere epilogue to the already conclusive victory. So Dtr., when dealing with the defeat of the Philistines by Samuel, makes this the last of a series of great deeds by "judges" in the "judges" period. Samuel's action had essentially the effect of reforming the people and thus opening the way for divine intervention. In vv.3-4, a passage closely related to Judg. 10:11-16 in subject matter and language, Dtr. speaks of the general conversion of the people through the agency of Samuel, relating this specifically to the first part of the ark story which is told immediately before (v.2). He goes on to describe the assembling of the army in Mizpah /34/ accompanied by fasting, confessions, sacrifices and prayers in sight of the assembling Philistines (vv.5-9), also in the style of the connecting passages in the book of Judges, and says that immediately after this the Philistines were defeated with the help of the panic caused by divine thunder /35/. Dtr. explicitly characterises this defeat as parallel to the Philistine victory of 1 Sam. 4 in speaking of the stone erected by Samuel near Mizpah /36/, according to local tradition, as a sign of victory, and making Samuel call it Ebenezer, a name taken from 4:1; 5:1. The consequences of the Mizpah victory are strongly emphasised in vv.13-14 /37/ and then Samuel's career as "judge" is narrated (vv.15-17), following the pattern used in the Jephthah story. No figure is given for his term of office /38/ - for reasons explained above /39/.

For Dtr. this is the end of the last "judges" story. Now, the people's demand for a king (1 Sam. 8) prepares the way for the period of the monarchy. Probably intentionally, Dtr. is only able to show imperfect motivation, based on the fact that Samuel was ageing and his sons /40/ were open to corruption. After all, God had hitherto always "raised up" a new "judge" at the right time. Dtr. simply traces the institution of the monarchy, of which he disapproves, back to the wicked self-will of the people who want to be like the other nations and no longer be forced to implore God in times of emergency to raise up a "judge" but rather to have someone in office continuously at their disposal. The function of the king is conceived as identical to that of "judging" as Dtr. conceives it in the "judges" period (cf. 8:5,6,20) except that the monarchy performs this function uninterruptedly and at its own discretion and not by the occasional specific commission of God /41/. This is how Dtr. depicts the incipient monarchy in 1 Sam. 8, composed in a thoroughly Deuteronomistic manner. Above all, he is interested in representing the demand for a monarchy as a refusal to be dependent on occasional divine help (v.7; cf. 10:19) and in representing the monarchy, responsible only to itself, as a burden on the people (vv.9-18), even if the people have yet to recognise it as such. Dtr. does so far follow the old tradition and its view of monarchy in having God empower Samuel to set up the monarchy in response to the demand of the people (vv.7,22a); and so after dispersing the elders who put to Samuel the demand for a king (8:22b), Dtr. has the opportunity to give the traditional text of the old story in which Samuel meets Saul and anoints him in private (9:1-10:16).

The old tradition of 9:1-10:16 was, indeed, uppermost in Dtr.'s mind when he inserted before the drawing of lots at Mizpah (10:17-27a) the scene between Samuel and the elders in 8:4-22 which has no particular place in the tradition /42/. In an independent narrative there would have been no reason here to divide the essentially homogeneous action into two scenes. This clearly demonstrates the dependence of 7:2-8:22, 10:17-27a and 12:1-25 on the old traditional account in 9:1-10:16 and 10:27b-11:15. Now 10:17-27a is certainly composed by Dtr., especially at the beginning, but Dtr.'s context does not seem to require it, since 9:15-16 and 10:1 established that God chose the first king and there was therefore no need to find out God's decision by drawing lots, even though Dtr. could have wanted this decision to be revealed before the public so that 11:14-15 would not look like an autonomous action of the people. This view may well have influenced Dtr. here. However, his main purpose in 10:17-27a is to find a place for a traditional story of Saul's accession, found in one of his sources which we do not know. Eissfeldt is obviously right in making the penetrating conjecture /43/ that 10:21b^b-27a contains a fragment of a story in which Saul was, by divine oracle, appointed king as the man marked out by his exceptional height /44/. But contrary to Eissfeldt's subsequent inference, 10:21b^b-27a is not part of an independent narrative. Such an inference cannot be proved and 10:21b^b-27a is so firmly integrated into Dtr.'s scheme that it is far more probably a fragment of a tradition adapted by Dtr. The passage 10:21b^b-27a would lack the necessary intro-duction and 10:17-21ab^b the necessary conclusion if they were seen as belonging to separate narratives. Furthermore, Dtr.'s location of the action in Mizpah, as early as v.17, probably comes from the tradition which he adapted /45/. Besides, the reference to the "rights and duties of the kingship" in 10:25a is inseparable from the "law of the king" in 8:9,11ff. This means that we are certainly not entitled to assume that 10:25a was added by Dtr. to the text of the old account /46/, but we may conclude that Dtr. took the theme of the proclamation of the "law of the king", which he develops independently in chapter 8, from the tradition which he adapted in chapter 10. Dtr. is probably following the literary model of Jos. 7:16ff. when he has Saul chosen by lot /47/ (1 Sam. 10:17) because he would have found the divine oracle that the tallest man be made king too primitive; so he keeps only the end of the old account which, surprisingly, says that Saul was in hiding. This story ended with the dispersal of the assembled people /48/ and it was, therefore, possible for Dtr. to insert 10:27b-11:15 without making any transition - this passage can be directly connected to 10:27a, a kind of historical answer to the doubt expressed there. We can assume only that Dtr. had this passage in view when he did not put Samuel's valedictory speech (chapter 12) immediately after the public election of Saul, which would have been the appropriate place for it (10:25a). Since 10:27b-11:15 led up to Saul's public proclamation as king /49/ this passage had to be put in before that valedictory speech which could then be easily brought in in connection with the assembly of the people in Gilgal (11:14-15).

In chapter 12 Dtr. makes Samuel's primary message to the people the assurance that, despite their ungodly demand for a king, they can still choose between obedience and disobedience and thus between preservation and annihilation - i.e., that despite the institution of the monarchy things can remain as they were before. In historical retrospect Samuel refers briefly to the liberation from Egypt /50/ and then at greater length to the time of the "judges". With regard to the latter (vv.9-11) he begins by citing the enemies, Sisera, the Philistines and Moab, which obviously refers us, in reverse order, to the "judges" Ehud, Shamgar and Deborah-Barak, and in v.11 the "judges" Gideon /51/, Jephthah and Samuel /52/ are mentioned by name. Whether or not it was a special literary "refinement" /53/ of Dtr. that this reference was divided into two sentences (necessarily corresponding to each other in content) and that the order in the first sentence was reversed, the fact remains that Dtr. wishes to remind us of <u>all</u> the "saviour" figures of the "judges" period /54/. It is curious that in v.12 the demand for a king is motivated by the threat of the Ammonite king Nahash which is not even mentioned in chapter 8. It is normally assumed that the two "sources" in 1 Sam. 7-12 are independent of each other and that 1 Sam. 12:12a^a was added later. Even disregarding this literary-critical assumption, it is advisable to delete this part-verse, because of chapter 8. However, to do so would make v.12a^{b}b follow v.11 very abruptly and so, bearing in mind the traditional text, we cannot justify the deletion and must assume that Dtr. was relatively late in taking note of the importance attributed in 10:27b-11:15 to the Ammonite threat, as part of the background to the monarchy. Perhaps it was only considerably later that this point, so easily associated with 8:5, occurred to Dtr. Thus 1 Sam. 12:12 would be a further proof that 7:2-8:22, 10:17-27a and 12:1-25 are independent of the account in 9:1-10:16 and 10:27b-11:15 /55/.

Therefore it was not without obvious effort and contrivance that Dtr. supplemented the old account which dealt favourably with the institution of the monarchy by adding long passages reflecting his disapproval of the institution. To this end he used an old tradition about Saul's accession, the existence of which seemed to give him a right to take certain liberties, to augment the text; and he went on to make great use of this right. Least compatible with the content of the old tradition was the representation of Samuel as "judge" in keeping with Dtr.'s general approach, even though here too Dtr. could use some elements from an old tradition about Samuel /56/.

To introduce the whole section Dtr. took over the old Samuel story 1 Sam. 1:1-4:12. We know that it was in Dtr. originally because he obviously derived from it (1:19; 2:11; 15:34 and passim) the information that Ramah was Samuel's home and native place (7:17; 8:4) to which he returned - this is tacitly assumed - after the loss of the Ark in Shiloh. This piece was originally a self-contained prophetic tradition /57/; its intention is indicated explicitly in 3:19-21. Before Dtr. it had already been augmented with all kinds of references to the worthlessness and wickedness of Eli's sons when they were priests in Shiloh and to their fate. Dtr. seems to have added only a few statements of his own, such as the characteristic reflection in 2:25b or 2:34-35 /58/ which is connected to the story he is about to tell in chapter 4 as a vaticinium ex eventu. This story fits into Dtr.'s plan as an introduction to Samuel, who is very important to him.

It is harder to decide whether Dtr.'s account included the Samson stories (Judg. 13:2-16:31) or whether they are a later interpolation. It is not crucial that the stories report no great victory for their hero and thus do not fit the plan used by Dtr. for his account of the "judges" period, since Dtr. does not seem pedantic enough to reject traditional material just because it is not easily integrated into a set pattern. Besides, the Samson stories may have helped Dtr. to fill up the first half of the 40 years of Philistine rule. Judg. 15:20 and 16:31b /59/ could also have come from Dtr. who might have varied the scheme after the Jephthah story and in view of the particular interest of the Samson story /60/. On the other hand, these statements are so similar to the later addition 1 Sam. 4:18b that they, like it, seem to be the work of a later author. Furthermore the Samson stories show no sign of having been worked on by Dtr. and since Samson's name is conspicuous by its absence in 1 Sam. 12:11, a passage which clearly aims to be comprehensive (vv.9-11), we must consider the possibility that the Samson stories were not added to Dtr.'s account until later. Then Dtr. could have followed Judg. 13:1 directly with 1 Sam. 1:1; as elsewhere he would have attached only one specified "saviour" figure to one specified period of foreign rule, in this case Samuel; indeed, the story of Samuel's origins went back before the beginning of the period of foreign rule as did the Jephthah story (Judg. 11:1-3).

Chapter Eight
SAUL, DAVID, SOLOMON

For the story of Saul and David Dtr. had access to an extensive collection of Saul-David traditions compiled long before Dtr. from different elements - the old tradition on Saul /1/ and, in particular, the story of the rise of David /2/ and the story of the Davidic succession /3/. As in the occupation story, the existence of this traditional material absolved Dtr. from the need to organise and construct the narrative himself. Once he has stated his fundamental position on the institution of the monarchy in no uncertain terms (1 Sam. 8-12), he has little need to interpose in the traditional account his own judgements and interpretations, particularly as the tradition itself gives a detailed account of the rapid downfall of Saul, the first king, notwithstanding his initial successes /4/, and as Dtr. is at one with the whole Old Testament tradition in seeing the figure of David, despite his weaknesses, as a model against which to judge the later Judaean kings /5/.

For the story of Saul, Dtr. simply reproduced the text of the remainder of the old Saul tradition (1 Sam. 13:2-16:13) and the first part of the story of the rise of David (1 Sam. 16:14ff.) which had already been attached to the Saul tradition; this takes him up to 2 Sam. 2:7. We see that the arrangement arose naturally out of the subject matter as he knew it, since in 1 Sam. 13:1 he inserts the formulaic introduction for Saul's reign /6/, and in 2 Sam. 2:10a-11 /7/ the formulaic introduction for the reign of Eshbaal /8/, along with the provisional introduction for David. Moreover there is no single clear sign that Dtr. edited the Saul story 1 Sam. 13:1-2 Sam. 2:7. On the one hand, 1 Sam. 13:7b-15a, which seems to have been added to the old account and was anticipated by the addition of 1 Sam. 10:8, shows no definite signs of having been worked on by Dtr. and most commentators do not regard it as Deuteronomistic /9/. On the other hand there is not a trace of Dtr. in 1 Sam. 14:47-51; this passage was certainly not part of the original Saul tradition but was later interpolated before the final sentence of 1 Sam. 14:52; but apart from the information on Saul's family in vv.49-51, surely a part of the tradition, it contains nothing but a very generalised reference to Saul's many and varied victories in vv.47-48 which is so inconsistent with Dtr.'s view of the first king that it can scarcely be attributed to him. Finally in 1 Sam. 15 the passage vv.24-31 was certainly added later but cannot be ascribed to Dtr. /10/ since his characteristic language and attitudes are not in evidence here.

After the formulaic Deuteronomistic introductions to Eshbaal and David (2 Sam. 2:10a-11), the extant version of the story of King David begins by following the remains of the traditional account of the rise of David and is subsequently based on the story of the succession. Here Dtr. intervenes only occasionally and even then contributes very little. After the old tradition had dealt with David's progress up to the unification of Israel and Judah under him /11/, Dtr. found it necessary to give the complete formulaic introduction to the reign of David (2 Sam. 5:4-5 /12/). In this context Dtr. altered the original, and historically appropriate, order of the final stages in the story of David's rise /13/ and immediately after the formulaic introduction reports the conquest of Jerusalem (vv.*6-12) /14/. Apparently he thought that this action of David was of paramount significance because it was then possible to recover the ark (which is so important for Dtr.), and the account of the decisive victory over the Philistines, therefore, takes second place /15/.

In Dtr.'s source this was followed by the end of the "ark story" and Nathan's prophecy associated with it. We cannot possibly claim that the latter section is Deuteronomistic /16/, since neither the prohibition of temple-building nor the strong emphasis on the value of the monarchy /17/ are in the spirit of Dtr. However it is quite conceivable that Dtr. did not completely refrain from adding corrective passages to this chapter with its fundamental statements on the interpretation of history. L. Rost's /18/ literary analysis of this chapter is along the right lines. He says that the original text, found in vv.1-7 and vv.11b,16,18-21,25-29 was added to later, the first addition being in vv.8-17; this expanded text existed before Dtr. who made two important alterations in keeping with his general approach. First, he inserted v.13a /19/, making the prohibition of temple-building apply to a particular time /20/, rather than being a matter of principle. Secondly, Rost /21/ is right to recognise that he inserted vv.22-24 which uses expressions from the preceding text /22/ regarding the promise made concerning the institution of the Davidic monarchy, and relates them to the Israelite nation of the past rather than the future. Looking back over the historical catastrophes of the eighth, seventh and sixth centuries B.C., Dtr. thought that this interpretation, running counter to the original meaning, was the only one possible /23/.

Recently, Alt /24/ has tried to explain 2 Sam. 8 as a continuation of 2 Sam. 5:17-25, and as the conclusion to the story of David's rise. But, as we have shown above, 2 Sam. 5:17-25 originally belonged not at the end of chapter 5 but before vv.6-10(12) /25/, and v.10(12) contains a literary conclusion which makes any kind of continuation of this strand of narrative quite unthinkable /26/. Rather we should look for signs of editorial activity by Dtr. in 2 Sam. 8, which now stands in isolation between different parts of the account of the Davidic succession. Making a direct connection with the important chapters 5-7 (David king of Judah and Israel, the conquest of Jerusalem, the transfer of the ark to Jerusalem, the question of building a temple) which belong to quite different literary contexts but are thematically apparently indivisible, Dtr. adds a general picture of David's successes in foreign affairs. For the end of 2 Sam. 8, that is, vv.15-18, cannot be taken in isolation from 2 Sam. 20:23-26 and 1 Kings 4:2-6. If 1 Kings 4:2-6 was taken over into the Solomon narrative by Dtr. who, as we can prove, had access to all kinds of information on the monarchic period in official records /27/, then the same must apply to the other two passages. In any case Dtr., on grounds of historical probability, would have assigned the two lists of officials in the Davidic period, one (as indicated in the introduction in v.15) to the beginning of David's reign, the other to its end; and this is why he puts the latter immediately before 1 Kings 1-1a. But if Dtr. attached 2 Sam. 8:15-18 to the David narrative, then he probably did the same, again after compiling official materials, with 8:1-14, and, in keeping with his usual manner of presenting such material, without adding anything himself apart from an inconsequential introductory sentence (v.1a^a) and a colourless formulaic conclusion (v.14b) /28/. In Dtr.'s source, 5:11 could have come next to 8:9-11, to which it is stylistically akin, but he would have put it after chapter 5 for the reasons given above.

Similarly, Dtr. made only slight alterations to the end of the story of David in 1 Kings 1:2 /29/. Apart from inserting a reference to the fulfilment of the prophecy in 1 Sam. 1-3 against the sons of Eli (2:27b), he merely augments David's last words to his son and successor with some general admonitions in the characteristic Deuteronomistic spirit (2:*2,3,4) /30/. Verse 4 is made to refer explicitly to Nathan's prophecy in words similar to those found in Dtr.'s account (1 Kings 8:25; 9:5). Furthermore (as Rost rightly observes /31/) Dtr. deviates very significantly from 2 Sam. 7: there righteousness on the part of future kings was assumed to be the rule (vv.14b-16); here it is described as the exception. Dtr. must be thinking of later developments in the monarchy as he saw them.

For Dtr., attempting to tell the story of King Solomon was quite a different matter from telling the stories of David and Saul, because the sources were completely different. For the latter he had access to a comprehensive and coherent narrative tradition, but for the former he had to construct his account out of diverse, disparate and hitherto scattered traditional material. In 1 Kings 11:41 he quotes as his main source the "Book of the Acts of Solomon". The terms in which he expresses this citation indicate that he extracted from the book what he thought important. This source contained the abundant official information which Dtr. is able to supply. We find not the actual official annals of the king but rather an adaptation of these accounts from an objective historical point of view, for the information is organised not according to year but according to subject, even if a subject has to extend over quite a number of years /32/. Even allowing for the possibility that Dtr. rearranged the material at certain points, we can get a rough idea of how "Book of the Acts of Solomon" was arranged. It detailed first the numerous buildings constructed by Solomon in the "city of Solomon" (cf. 6; 7:1-12) and the bronze artefacts made for these (7:13-46), then the "forced labour" instituted in connection with the buildings (cf. *9:15-23) and then the putting to use of the new buildings (cf. 9:24; *8:1-13; 9:25) /33/. Then it reported that Solomon organised trading expeditions on the Red Sea (9:26-28; 10:11-12), that he amassed treasures, especially of gold (10:14-22), and traded in war horses and war chariots (10:26-29). This seems more or less how the "Book of the Acts of Solomon" at Dtr.'s disposal was arranged; of course we cannot rule out the possibility that it contained all manner of material which Dtr. did not use. In addition Dtr. had access to some anecdotes about Solomon and to various sources covering some of the details. The picture of Solomon which Dtr. fashions out of this material is certainly not without its contradictions. On one hand Dtr. had to see the building of the Jerusalem temple which, according to the Deuteronomic law, God had "chosen" for his "name" as a holy place, as a beneficial enterprise, and its completion as the whole purpose of the first period of the monarchy. On the other hand, the disintegration of the Davidic kingdom after Solomon's death seems to show that the turn for the worse, which was the hallmark of the later monarchy, must have begun in Solomon's lifetime. Dtr. tried to overcome this difficulty by dividing the story of Solomon into two separate phases. At the beginning of each God appears to Solomon at Gibeon (1 Kings 3:4-15 and 9:1-9). Dtr. lays stress upon the first phase, in which Solomon's ways were pleasing to God, while explicitly describing his later moral deterioration as a manifestation of old age (11:4). Once we see this, it is easy to understand the structure of the story of Solomon in Dtr.'s version.

The beginnings of the story of Solomon were already dealt with in the traditional story of the Davidic succession. Dtr. introduces his own account of Solomon with the acknowledgement in 3:3a, admittedly qualified in 3:3b /34/. Then comes the traditional story, eminently suitable for an introduction, of the vision of God at Gibeon, in which Solomon is promised wealth and glory as well as the wisdom for which he asked (3:4-15) and the likewise traditional story of the judgement of Solomon which serves as the first concrete evidence of the king's wisdom (3:16-28). Dtr. makes no change in this section, except at the end of the Gibeon story where he cites the basic conditions for God's benevolence (v.14) which Solomon later ignores - and makes Solomon perform his concluding thank-offering, not at Gibeon, as the source clearly intended /35/, but in Jerusalem before "the ark of the covenant of Yahweh" /36/ (v.15b^a). The introduction also includes the details of Solomon's system of government, based on the official records at Dtr.'s disposal (4:1-5:8): the list of his high officials (4:2-6), the list of the administrators and their provinces (4:7-19) /37/ together with added details on the function of these officers (4:20; 5:8) /38/.

Then Dtr. appropriately introduces the main part of his account of Solomon, the story of the building of the temple, with a portion of old narrative on the king's extraordinary wisdom (5:9-14). But before he reports the actual building, he describes the preparations in some detail; I see no reason to doubt that the whole section 5:15-32 is by Dtr. From the old notice in 2 Sam. 5:11 and the information given in the "Book of the Acts of Solomon" on King Hiram of Tyre's participation in

Solomon's maritime activities (9:27; 10:11,22), Dtr. inferred that
if Hiram helped to build David's palace he must certainly have
helped Solomon to build the temple /39/; and in fact Solomon
could not have obtained the cedar which he needed for his
buildings except by negotiating an agreement with the
Phoenicians /40/. Dtr. introduces Solomon's dealings with Hiram
(v.15b) by alluding to 2 Sam. 5:11 and then Solomon supports his
case by referring to the prophecy of Nathan as Dtr. understood
it and as 2 Sam. 7:13a explains it (vv.17-19). The details of the
arrangements made (vv.20-23) /41/ need not be based on any
particular source since Dtr. had only to take account of the
normal and sensible practice of floating in wood from the
Lebanon; and one cannot be sure, to say the least, whether the
official sources known to Dtr. told him the extent of Solomon's
exports to Hiram (vv.24-25) or whether he invented the figures.
Similarly, the passage on the organisation of forced labour
(vv.27-32) is entirely by Dtr. - except for the later additions -
and we cannot know what, if any, source he had for the figures
given here; the figures seem remarkably high for data from an
authentic source. Moreover, Dtr. has ignored the constitutional
limits to the king's power and deviated from the official
tradition in letting Solomon levy forced labour from the whole
of Israel (9:20-22), determining their work with reference to
v.20a (v.28a) and taking the statement in v.28b from 4:6b;
meanwhile v.30, the introduction to which shows it is simply a
comment in passing, is taken over with a change in the numbers
from 9:23. In vv.31-32 it is typical of Dtr. to think only of the
building of the temple whereas the "Book of the Acts of
Solomon" had in view all of Solomon's buildings. Dtr. has taken
over the detailed report of the building of the temple in chapter
6 from the "Book of the Acts of Solomon" and, on the basis of
6:37, introduced the report with the note on chronology which
contains the figure 480 (discussed in detail above, pp.18ff.)
/42/. Following the account of the temple building Dtr. made
detailed use of the source material concerning the building of
the "House of the Forest of Lebanon" (7:2-5) because this
building contained Solomon's famous golden shields (10:17)
mentioned again later (14:26). In contrast Dtr. refers to each of
the other buildings only by quoting the first sentence
concerning it in his source (7:6a,6b,7,8a,8b); and 7:1a looks as if
it originally formed part of the introduction to the section
dealing with all the buildings of Solomon's city. This would
suggest that Dtr. went against the order in his source and put

the building of the temple at the beginning, a procedure quite consistent with his interests. Afterwards Dtr. draws on the "Book of the Acts of Solomon" to report the bronze-work done specifically for the temple /43/ and then, after indicating how much bronze was used in the work (7:47), he adds his own inventory of the gold used in the temple (7:48-50) /44/ and a concluding sentence on the transfer of the treasures of David's sanctuary (cf. 2 Sam. 8:11) into the newly built temple (7:51).

Dtr. seems to have regarded the dedication of the temple as Solomon's next most urgent task; therefore he took from a later section of the "Book of the Acts of Solomon" /45/ the old account of the temple building (8:1a^a,2a^{a}b,3,5,*6,[7,8/46/] 12,13) and supplemented this with statements of his own. He says that the bringing of the "ark of the covenant of Yahweh" /47/ into the new temple was the most important event (v.1b) and took place in the presence of the entire population (v.2a^a) and that this "shrine" was explicitly entrusted to the "levitical priests" (v.4b); he reminds us that the ark contained the two tablets from Horeb /48/ (v.9) /49/. Most important, Dtr. attaches to the old traditional formula of dedication spoken by Solomon the long prayer of dedication by Solomon which, as part of Dtr.'s overall design, characterises the completion of the temple as a milestone in his narrative - for the content of this prayer, see the detailed discussion below, pp.93f. To this prayer he prefixes introductory remarks by Solomon (8:14-21) which refer once again to Nathan's prophecy, as understood and developed by Dtr., and conclude by declaring the temple the dwelling-place of the ark. The prayer itself (8:22-53) /50/, begins by referring back to 2:4 and therefore to the reinterpretation of Nathan's prophecy found there (v.25) /51/. After the prayer comes the blessing (in 8:54-61) which speaks of God's past deeds (v.56) - cf. in particular Jos. (21:44f.) 23:1,14 - and then the account of the ritual completion of the dedication (8:62-66).

After Solomon has accomplished his main task in this way, Dtr. makes God appear to Solomon at Gibeon again (9:1-9) /52/ on the analogy of the traditional story of 3:4-15; in this vision, coming in response to the prayer of dedication /53/, God warns Solomon severely against future apostasy and threatens to destroy people and temple if this warning is not heeded. This introduces the second part of the story of Solomon, the beginning of his apostasy. First Dtr. tells a traditional aetiological story centred on the name Cabul which he supplies

with a context: Solomon fails to pay Hiram back properly
(9:10-14); in Dtr.'s view this incident is obviously the first blot
on Solomon's image. It is true that Dtr. follows this immediately with the rest of the material which he wished to relate
from the "Book of the Acts of Solomon" and in the order given
there - i.e. the forced labour (9:15a,20-23) /54/, the remaining
information on the putting to use of the new buildings (9:24-25)
/55/, the review of the maritime activities undertaken by
Solomon and Hiram (9:26-28; 10:11-12), with which Dtr.
associates the traditional anecdote of the visit of the queen of
Sheba, as a further illustration of the influx of wealth from
exotic foreign lands during Solomon's reign (10:1-10,13) and
finally the results of these mercantile enterprises - the golden
ornaments made at the command of Solomon (10:14-22) /56/ and
Solomon's trade in war horses and war chariots (10:26-29) /57/.
However, Dtr. now goes on to relate his own story of Solomon's
apostasy (11:1-13). He took the material for this from 2 Kings
23:13 which mentions the "high places" which Solomon built east
of Jerusalem (for the foreigners at his court and among his
officers) in honour of the gods of the Sidonians, Moabites and
Ammonites. Dtr. develops this into a report that Solomon's
foreign wives seduced him into worshipping the "other gods"
which is said to have caused him to build these cultic places
during his old age. As a result of this apostasy God became
angry and threatened to deprive Solomon of his kingdom. In
Dtr.'s view (cf. 2:4; 8:25) Solomon ought to have felt the full
impact of this punishment immediately: it was only out of
consideration for his father David's good conduct and for
Jerusalem as the site of the new sanctuary that the punishment
did not start until after Solomon's death and even then was
mitigated so that David's descendants retained part of David's
kingdom; this was in fact what happened historically.

Thereafter Dtr. gives some valuable historical information on
various domestic and foreign problems during Solomon's reign;
his source is unknown. He puts this information at the end of his
account of Solomon, in keeping with his plan that the reign of
this king should be made up of first a longer and more
successful period, characterised by conduct pleasing to God,
and then a shorter period /58/ characterised by apostasy and
misfortune; even though the events described here begin earlier
(11:21) and their consequences can be felt throughout much of
Solomon's reign (11:25a^a). The strange order in vv.23-25
seems to suggest that Dtr. wanted to put the events in

chronological order. Hence he began with the story of Hadad (11:14-22) which started quite a long time before, broke off to give the story of Rezon (11:23-25a^a), then concluded the Hadad story (11:25a^{b}b), here in an apparently abbreviated form which is now textually misplaced (cf. v.25a^b) /59/. This is followed by a story, from the same old source, about Jeroboam, who does not reach his full prominence until after Solomon's death (11:26-28,40). After this Dtr. appropriately begins the prophetic story of "Jeroboam and Ahijah the Shilonite" /60/ (11:29a^{b}b /61/ to 31, 36ab^a /62/ and 37 /63/) and supplements this account with his own work: a long explanation for the continuing allegiance of one tribe and one tribe only /64/ to the dynasty of David and linking it with 11:1-13 (11:32-35) /65/ by means of an ill-fitting addition on the name Jerusalem (11:36b^b) and an admonition to Jeroboam to walk in the ways of the divine law (11:38,39a) /66/. Then Dtr. ends his account with the formulaic conclusion (11:41-43) which he always uses henceforth to mark the end of a king's reign /67/.

Chapter Nine
THE PERIOD OF THE KINGS OF ISRAEL AND JUDAH

It is general knowledge that Dtr. based the last part of his history on the "Books of the Chronicles of the Kings of Israel" and the "Books of the Chronicles of the Kings of Judah". These sources provided him with the material for a framework for his portrayal of this period. We can be sure that these "Books of the Chronicles" are derived from the official annals of the Israelite and Judaean kings, but on the other hand are not to be identified with them, but rather seen as unofficial histories of the kings adapted from official material; we can also see that the "Book of the Acts of Solomon" is a similar history of that king adapted from official sources /1/. Like the "Book of the Acts of Solomon" these "Books of the Chronicles" were, clearly, written at a time when the period which they treated was already over and done with, whereas the official annals must have been composed while the events were still happening /2/. We are not concerned to trace the development of the official annals into the "Books of the Chronicles" directly used by Dtr. and in any case this cannot be done conclusively /3/. Rather, we are trying to ascertain what Dtr.'s intentions were in his use of the "Books of the Chronicles". He himself remarks repeatedly that he has taken only certain specific details from the "Books of the Chronicles" and that the reader can find the rest of the information on the "acts" of each particular king in the "Books of the Chronicles" for himself. His intention then - and this is ✻ absolutely crucial to any evaluation of his work - is to write not the history of individual kings but the history of the whole monarchical period, the catastrophic end of which was evident. He is commonly criticised for misunderstanding and, as a result, misevaluating the historical significance of various kings - but we can see that this criticism does not apply in so far as he set out to describe not the acts of individual kings /4/ but the history of the monarchy as a whole in this section of his history; and the outcome is not affected by the positive achievements of individual kings. Given this approach, we can understand his judgement on the kings. The repetitive monotony of these judgements merely shows that he is really attempting a verdict on the whole monarchical period. Certainly there are some exceptions to the unfavourable judgement he passes. However, they are qualified and isolated and serve only to suggest that the monarchy per se could have been a positive factor in Israel's history but in fact served only as a catalyst in its downfall /5/. Of course the criteria for each judgement are Dtr.'s own, and so are determined by the conditions of his own time /6/ and cannot be regarded as historically infallible, but the generally negative character of his judgements arose from Dtr.'s consistent view of this period, which he deals with as a single unit /7/.

In keeping with Dtr.'s intention to describe the monarchical period as a whole, he has used the "Books of the Chronicles" as his primary source for the chronological framework. It is true that Dtr. attempted to provide his whole history with a firm chronological structure, the lengths of reigns and dates of events in both kingdoms forming the only means of establishing an unbroken, continuous connection between the dynasties of Israel and Judah. Dtr. nevertheless chose not to produce an internally connected history of the whole of the period of the monarchy, perhaps because he did not have enough traditional material. In any case he decidedly did not intend to relate the "acts" of the kings fully. This means that all the historical detail in the "Books of the Chronicles" has been lost but, as a compensation, Dtr. has transmitted the equally valuable chronological material from the "Books of the Chronicles" and thus, indirectly, from the official annals of the kings.

Apart from the chronological framework, Dtr. has taken little from the "Books of the Chronicles". The history of the kings of Israel has been drastically shortened because Dtr. regards it as nothing but a rapid progression towards the annihilation which took place a mere two centuries after Solomon's death, and which was survived by nothing worth mentioning of the old order. This carefully tailored account of the succession of kings with its chronological structure also includes isolated references to the various usurpations in 1 Kings 15:27,28; 16:9-12; 16:15-18,21,22 /8/; 2 Kings 15:10; 15:14,16; 15:25; 15:30a. In their context, these contain various important pieces of information on the specific historical situation. Although Dtr. tells us little of the history of the kings, he does tell it in the appropriate historical context and, by giving us the information mentioned above, rounds out the picture of the Israelite succession. Moreover he reports these usurpations in order to show us the rapid decline of the monarchy in Israel; with his Judaean viewpoint, he did not see the objective background to these usurpations, namely the element of charismatic leadership which characterised the Israelite monarchy. As an anchor for the data of the chronological framework, Dtr. also excerpted, from the "Books of the Chronicles", details of the changing seat of government of the kings of Israel (1 Kings 12:25; 16:24) /9/. To establish its relevance to the earlier part of his history, Dtr. reported the reconstruction of Jericho as a royal city and refers to Jos. 6:26 (1 Kings 16:34). Dtr. has in mind the Elijah and Elisha stories which he plans to tell in detail when he reports from the "Books of the Chronicles" King Ahab's marriage to Jezebel (1 Kings 16:31b^b) and introduces it with an emphatic statement (v.31a) and a factually incorrect concluding statement (v.31b^a). The interest in prophecies, which is conspicuous in Dtr.'s comprehensive stories about the prophets, motivates Dtr. to quote the "Books of the Chronicles" at 2 Kings 14:25; here the prophet Jonah proclaimed to Jeroboam II that the former borders of the state of Israel would be restored; and this announcement was in fact realised. In vv.26-27, Dtr. explains this event in accordance with his theological interpretation of history, saying that God in his mercy wanted to give Israel a respite, and in the absence of other means /10/ - Dtr. must have in mind some of the Elisha stories he has just told - used the present king as a "saviour" /11/. To the theme of the fall of Israel belongs the report of King Menahem's payment of tribute to the Assyrian emperor (2 Kings 15:19-20) and the short but pregnant reference to the events of 733 (15:29).

As far as I can see, this is all that Dtr. took from the "Books of the Chronicles of the Kings of Israel" - except for the reference to the "ivory house" built by Ahab which he includes for its intrinsic interest but only as part of his conventional reference to the "Books of the Chronicles" without quoting the text of his source itself (1 Kings 22:39). This probably indicates that he kept strictly to a plan in making his excerpts from the "Books of the Chronicles", and thus when he includes something which seems to him extraneous but interesting he does so only in note form.

Dtr. took rather more from the "Books of the Chronicles of the Kings of Judah". In particular he used anything of relevance to the temple in Jerusalem. We see this as early as 1 Kings 14:25-28 which is not so much about the Palestinian campaign of the Egyptian pharaoh Shishak /12/ as about Rehoboam's payment of tribute to Shishak who, as a result, spared Judah and Jerusalem. The tribute had to be paid not only from the treasury of the king's palace but also from those of the temple; in addition, Solomon's golden shields had to be given over. Thereafter, when the king entered the temple his retinue bore bronze rather than golden shields. Apart from 15:12-13 /13/, of course, what follows (15:16-22) also has to do with the temple. Here King Asa must again use the treasures of the temple and the palace for a gift to the Aramaean king Benhadad (v.18), in order to exercise influence at a crucial moment /14/. In the history of King Joash, we can cite not only the obvious example of 2 Kings 12:5-17 but also 2 Kings 12:18-19 which tells how the Aramaean king Hazael was bribed to withdraw by a tribute consisting of the votive gifts dedicated by the kings and of all the gold remaining in the temple and palace. Dtr. took the history of the war between Judah and Israel in 2 Kings 14:8-14 from the Judaean "Books of Chronicles" /15/ because this war culminated in the plundering of the temple and palace. Because this story contains an allusion to King Amaziah's successful campaign against Edom (v.10), Dtr. completed the picture by quoting, in addition, the notes in 14:7 and 14:22 from the "Books of the Chronicles". The information in 2 Kings 15:35b and the story in 2 Kings 16:7-18 also concern the temple; to explain the facts of the latter Dtr. quite correctly introduces it with material from the "Books of the Chronicles", 16:5 and 16:6 /16/. Furthermore, the temple is the subject matter of 2 Kings 18:4b and 18:13-16 /17/ in which the famous tribute to Sennacherib was again at the expense of the treasure in the temple and palace and even the gold overlay on the doors and door frames (?) of the temple; it is understandable that Dtr. needed 18:13-16 to introduce the series of stories about Isaiah which follow. After this, naturally enough, Dtr. gives a long report, going back ultimately to the official annals but taken from the "Books of the Chronicles", of the measures adopted by Josiah with regard to the cult (2 Kings 23:4-15,19-20a). Finally, when he adds the account of the first conquest of Jerusalem by Nebuchadnezzar (2 Kings 24:10-16), he is primarily interested in reporting what happened to the temple treasure. Apart from a few pleasant exceptions, Dtr.'s history of the temple in the period of the monarchy, drawn from "Books of the Chronicles" of the kings of Judah, is primarily of how the temple was stripped of its wealth by its own kings; and he must have seen this as a sure sign of progressive decay.

For the Judaean kings, Dtr. uses the "Books of the

Chronicles" not only for chronological information but also for the necessary information on the succession of rulers. Examples are Athaliah's usurpation, her fall and the installation of Joash in 2 Kings 11:1-20; the remarks on the murder of Joash and its consequences in 2 Kings 12:21-22; 14:5; the assassination of Amaziah and the accession of Azariah/Uzziah in 2 Kings 14:19-21; the illness of Azariah and the regency of Jotham in 2 Kings 15:5; the information on the murder of Amon and the installation of Josiah in 2 Kings 21:23-24; the death of Josiah in battle and the accession of Jehoahaz in 2 Kings 23:29-30 /18/; the intervention of the pharaoh Neco in the succession in 2 Kings 23:33-35; and finally the installation of Zedekiah by the king of Babylon in 2 Kings 24:17.

This accounts for virtually all the material which Dtr. took from the Judaean "Books of the Chronicles"; any other material taken from this source Dtr. uses for different and at all times obvious reasons. For example, in 1 Kings 22:48-50 he reports Jehoshaphat's unsuccessful attempt to restore sea trade with Ophir, as a sequel to the story of Solomon and also as a vivid illustration of the decline of the monarchy since Solomon. Similarly, when Dtr. mentions the renewed revolt of the Edomites /19/ in 2 Kings 8:20-22 he does so deliberately, in order to supply a thematically necessary link between the passage under discussion and the note in 2 Kings 14:7 /20/ which he needed for other reasons. When he goes on to refer to the revolt of the city of Libnah, he is evidently following his source but could well be citing a symptom of the continuing decline. In addition the annalistic report of the downfall of the state of Israel and the deportation of the upper classes must by its nature have a Judaean source. These events are summarised in the section on the reign of the Judaean king of that time, Hezekiah (2 Kings 18:9-11). The Judaean annals of the kings would doubtless have treated these events because of their prime importance for Judah and they would have been reported in the "Books of the Chronicles of the Kings" which was in course of compilation. However, Dtr. has anticipated this report, almost word for word, as early as 2 Kings 17:5-6 - the section on the reign of Hoshea had to deal with the end of the state of Israel. Before this he has told us something of Hoshea's previous treachery, which, given the reference to the pharaoh's name, he could not have made up himself but perhaps took from the "Books of the Chronicles of the Kings of Israel" /21/. Finally he could use the "Books of the Chronicles" as his source in 2 Kings 24:1-2a^a /22/ to prepare the way for 2 Kings 24:10-16 and in 2 Kings 24:7 which is needed to link 23:33-35 with 24:10ff. On the other hand, he obviously had no official annals at his disposal to help him describe the downfall of the Judaean state; he had to use some other source /23/. In the final sentence on Hezekiah, 2 Kings 20:20, Dtr. refers to the building of the water-tunnel in Jerusalem, because of its intrinsic interest to him, but keeps the reference brief since it is not related to the subjects which he has set out to treat in his account of the monarchical period /24/.

In his history of the monarchical period Dtr. has made extensive use of stories about the prophets. The prophets, "men of God", appear chiefly as opponents to the kings and surely Dtr. meant them to be understood in this way. They confront those rulers who are apostates, or inclined to apostasy, with an unambiguous statement of the word and will of God. First, we have some narrative cycles, each of which accumulated around one prophetic figure and was handed down in the circles of homines religiosi. Much space is given to the Elijah and Elisha cycle which is made up of originally independent episodes and a short series of anecdotes, welded together into a more or less unified continuous narrative before Dtr.'s time. Dtr. incorporated it into his history, splitting it up into parts /25/. Similarly, Dtr. had access to the Isaiah cycle as a composite whole made up of separate elements.

There are other stories about the prophets which, in the same way as a series of Elisha stories, stress the intervention of a prophet in domestic or foreign affairs. Often these affairs are described at great length and sometimes the figure of the prophet, although still the mainspring of the action, disappears from the picture completely. The first example of this is the story of the prophet Ahijah of Shiloh which is complete in itself and more comprehensive than is normally supposed; it accompanies the rise of King Jeroboam I. It begins in 1 Kings 11:29a^{b}b-31,36ab^a-37 with a meeting between the prophet and the future king who receives a promise that he will rule over ten Israelite tribes. It goes on to explain in detail how this promise was fulfilled (1 Kings 12:1-20) /26/ and how Jeroboam forsook the path of righteousness by setting up "golden calves" in Bethel and Dan (12:26-31) /27/ with the result that the same Ahijah of Shiloh, when consulted about Jeroboam's sick son, had to prophesy not only the boy's death but also the destruction of Jeroboam and his house, which would come about as certainly as the death of the son, which, in fulfilment of the prophecy, occurred immediately. So ends this story (1 Kings 14:1-18). The wording of 12:19 indicates that the story was written down before the end of the state of Israel. Then we have the story of the prophet Micaiah ben Imlah and the fulfilment of his prophecy to King Ahab (1 Kings 22:2b-37). This story is linked with 1 Kings 20 through the introductory words of vv.1-2a /28/. 1 Kings 20 and 22 could scarcely have belonged together in the first place, since 1 Kings 20 stands in sharp contrast to 1 Kings 22; the former is a series of anecdotes about prophets, brought into the historical context of the Aramaean wars of King Ahab; these anecdotes give no names for the various "prophet(s)" and "men of God" and "prophetic disciples". It is more likely that the self-contained story of Micaiah ben Imlah was later prefaced by an amalgam of various prophetic stories of different kinds which accompany part of the history of Ahab's Aramaean wars /29/. However, the link between 1 Kings 20 and 1 Kings 22 certainly existed before Dtr. There are grounds for believing that the story of the anointing of Jehu by one of Elisha's "prophetic disciples" and of the accession of Jehu to the kingship (2 Kings 9:1-10:27) is not from the cycle of stories about Elijah and Elisha, since here Elisha is very much in the background, and that, instead, the stories of the prophets' interventions in the succession of Israelite kings and dynasties formed a cycle of their own. In that case, 1 Kings *11,*12,*14 and 1 Kings (20) 22 and 2 Kings 9-10 would have belonged to this cycle; but it cannot be proved since these sections are not specifically linked with each other and they have in common only the subject and the idea of the word of the prophet and of its effect.

We must now consider briefly how Dtr. has used the sources available to him to construct his presentation of the history of the monarchical period.

First, with a link to one element in his material on Solomon (1 Kings 11:26-28,40), he inserts the Ahijah story and makes his own additions to it /30/. Then, after the final reference to Solomon, he appropriately continues the Ahijah story /31/ and does not bring in the brief reference from the "Books of the Chronicles" to the seats of government under Jeroboam until just before the climax of this story (12:25). Then he interrupts the Ahijah story again with a long insertion, for, after mentioning the state sanctuary of Bethel which Jeroboam built, he is prompted to append a local prophetic story, indigenous to

Bethel, and told there after King Josiah had desecrated the famous sanctuary of Bethel. According to this, when Jeroboam I celebrated the first great autumn festival in his new state sanctuary and himself officiated as priest before the altar /32/, a "man of God" from Judah - Josiah too was later to come from Judah - predicted that this sanctuary would be destroyed later. The man's grave could be pointed out in Bethel because he never returned home but met a strange end on the outskirts of Bethel. This long and detailed prophetic story was clearly known to Dtr. as a separate entity; he used it because it relates directly to the work of King Josiah, which was so very important to him. Dtr. incorporated the end of the story, in which the prophecy of the "man of God" is fulfilled and Josiah spares his grave, into the official report of Josiah's entry into Bethel (2 Kings 23:16-18) /33/. After a transition /34/, the rest of the Ahijah story follows in 14:1-18 /35/.

The conclusion of the account of Jeroboam (14:19-20) /36/ is followed by the sections on the first three Judaean kings up to and including Asa, who were contemporary with Jeroboam. In keeping with Dtr.'s practice from that point on each section is given as a complete entity from beginning to end; for example, the section on the long reign of Asa (15:9-24) reports his quarrel with King Baasha of Israel, even though Baasha is not treated until 16:1-16. In the section on Rehoboam (14:21-31) Dtr. not only couples the first reference to Jerusalem as seat of the Judaean kings with the formula which he normally attaches to the name "Jerusalem" (v.21), but also, at the point where the short verdict on the king in question is regularly given, he refers at great length to the cultic sins committed in Judah as well, vv.22-24. He goes on to make a general comment on the cult practices in Judah of the sort which the Ahijah story implicitly makes on conduct in the state of Israel. Over and above the usual basic material, the sections on Rehoboam, Abijam (15:1-8) /37/ and Asa (15:9-24) /38/ contain only a few excerpts from the "Books of the Chronicles of the Kings" and these we have already discussed.

Dtr. followed the section on the long reign of Asa with sections on the Israelite kings contemporary with him up to and including Ahab. In the section on Nadab 15:25-31(32), Dtr. inserted a reference to the threat Ahijah made to Jeroboam which is now carried out (vv.29-30). In the account of Baasha (15:33-16:7) Dtr. derives from a note in the "Books of the Chronicles" (16:12) the fact that a prophet called Jehu issued a threat to this king; then, in 16:1-4, he freely employs this threat, using elements of the Ahijah story (14:7,10,11) /40/, in order to offer a similar explanation for the fall of the house of Baasha as the Ahijah story gave for the fall of the house of Jeroboam. The sections on Elah (16:8-14), Zimri (16:15-20 with an appendix, vv.21-22) and Omri (16:23-28), contain within the usual framework some excerpts from the "Books of the Chronicles" which we have already discussed. In the section on Ahab (16:29ff.) the stereotyped introductory sentence and a few pieces of information from the "Books of the Chronicles" /39/ are appropriately followed by the first of the Elijah stories, in their traditional wording (1 Kings 17-19) /41/. However, Dtr. has put the Elijah-story of Naboth's vineyard together with the prophecy of Ahab's death (chapter 21) immediately before chapter 22, and hence has isolated chapter 20, placing it between the Elijah stories /42/. In chapter 21 Dtr. adds to the prophecy of Ahab's death (v.19) a passage of his own (vv.21-22,24-26) /43/ which looks beyond Ahab's personal fate to the fate of his dynasty /44/ and speaks of it in terms similar to those in 16:4, using expressions taken from the Ahijah story in 14:10-11 and, finally (vv.25-26), presenting Ahab as a symptom of the continually intensifying moral degeneration. The prophetic story in 22:1-38 /45/ is followed immediately by the formulaic conclusion to the story of Ahab (22:39-40).

After continuing the Judaean succession with the section on Jehoshaphat (22:41-51) /46/, Dtr. returns to the Israelite succession. Here he had to accommodate the rest of the Elijah-Elisha story. 2 Kings 1:2-17a[a], originally handed down without the name of a king, was applied by Dtr. to Ahab's successor Ahaziah, since, coming as it did after 1 Kings 22, it could not refer to Ahab, and it provides most of the content of the section on this king (1 Kings 22:52 - 2 Kings 1:18) /47/. In accordance with the traditional arrangement of the Elijah-Elisha stories, Elisha does not begin public life until the translation of Elijah, the account of which comes between sections on two different kings in 2 Kings 2 with two short anecdotes about Elisha appended to it. Dtr. had therefore no choice but to include most of the Elisha stories in the section on King Jehoram (2 Kings 3:1ff.), using the traditional wording and probably also the traditional arrangement /48/ (2 Kings 3:4-8:15). This is facilitated by the fact that the name of the first king with whom Elisha is connected is not mentioned anywhere in the stories /49/. After this Dtr. finds it necessary to continue the list of Judaean kings with sections on Jehoram (8:16-24) /50/ and Ahaziah (8:25-27). Then in 8:28-29 he was able to include sentences, simply borrowed from 9:15a,16b, to introduce the long story in 2 Kings 9:1-10:27.

Dtr. alters the actual story of Jehu's accession (9:1-10:27) /51/ only slightly, by repeating 1 Kings 21:21-22a in 9:8b,9, by referring to 9:36 in 9:10a and by mentioning Elijah by name in 10:10b. He passes over without comment the fact that 9:25,26,36 contain allusions to stories about Elijah, stories which he probably did not know and certainly did not use, and also variants of 1 Kings 21. On the other hand he probably added the final reflection in 10:28-33 that Jehu did well to remove "the Baal" but that it was his own conduct which brought about the oppression by King Hazael of Damascus foretold by Elisha (8:12). The Aramaean oppression began as early as Jehu's time (v.32), but after the formulaic conclusion to the reign of Jehu (10:34-36) /52/, Dtr. next deals with several events in Judah contemporary with Jehu (the reign and downfall of Athaliah, 11:1-20; section on Joash, 12:1-22); these use extensive excerpts from the "Books of the Chronicles". Only after this does Dtr. proceed to supply more detail about the Aramaean oppression, in sections on the Israelite kings Jehoahaz (13:1-9) and Jehoash (13:10-25). These sections link on to the account of the death of Elisha (13:14-19, with appendix vv.20-21), which Dtr. places in the reign of Jehoash, although, in the original tradition, the king is not named /53/; and he includes it most remarkably <u>after</u> the formulaic conclusion to the reign of Jehoash (13:12-13 /54/). From this story Dtr. inferred that the Aramaean oppression still continued (13:3,7) /55/ but that, under Jehoash, God had promised a "saviour" (13:4-5) - and this probably meant the dying Elisha - and that, after the death of Hazael, Jehoash succeeded in defeating the Aramaeans (13:22-25). Then Dtr. alternates between the Judaean and Israelite sequence of kings with sections on, first, Amaziah of Judah (14:1-22) /56/, then Jeroboam II of Israel (14:23-29) then Azariah/Uzziah of Judah (15:1-7) and then the Israelite successors of Jeroboam (15:8-31) /57/.

The chapters on the Judaean kings Jotham (15:32-38) and Ahaz (16:1-20) mark the transition to Dtr.'s account of the historical complexities which led to the end of the state of Israel. We cannot say for certain why he dates the beginnings of what is called the Syro-Ephraimite war, which according to 16:5ff. happened under Ahaz, as early as the time of Jotham

(15:37) /58/. In any case, Dtr. justifiably saw the surrender of Ahaz to the Assyrians as a parallel to the destruction of the Israelite state /59/ which was Israel's own fault. In the lengthy reflections on the causes of the latter event (17:7ff.), the language and ideas of which are typical of Dtr., Judah is included (v.13), and at the end (vv.18b-20) /60/ Dtr. associates the fate of the Judaean state with that of the Israelite state, seeing both as deliverance "into the hand of spoilers". He links the notes from the "Books of the Chronicles" (17:24,29-31) with another piece of local cult history from Bethel (17:25-28), and refers again to the religious conditions in the former kingdom of Israel (17:32-34a) /61/. Then he represents the period of King Hezekiah (18:1-20:21) in which he appropriately sets the Isaiah cycle (18:17-20:19) /62/ as nothing but a transitory interlude, although Hezekiah gets special praise for his religious measures /63/. In his account of Manasseh (21:1-18) on the other hand, Dtr. becomes more specific, including not just his usual statements but also a few details from 23:4ff. and Deut. 18:10f.; here he is clearly thinking of 17:7ff. and in v.13 he explicitly sets up a parallel between the imminent fate of the state of Judah and the accomplished fate of the state of Israel.

It is true that before the fate of the Judaean state is accomplished, the reign of King Josiah (22:1-23:30) /64/ supplies an element of retardation. Inevitably this reign was of particular significance to Dtr. because in it that law which he has placed at the beginning of his history as the authentic exposition of the Sinai decalogue was found in the temple and put into practice by the king /65/. Hence, immediately after the formulaic introduction to the section on Josiah (22:1-2), Dtr. reports the finding of the law (22:3-23:3); his account is probably based on an official record of this important event /66/. Dtr. follows this in 23:4-20a with excerpts from the "Books of the Chronicles" on Josiah's religious measures, which, by their position, are made to look like a mere execution of the prescriptions of this newly discovered law, although this is, in fact, the case for only some of the measures. Finally, 23:20b serves as a transition to the section 23:21-27 which was added by Dtr. and is meant to supply further material on the execution of the law, which Dtr. considers worth mentioning over and above the excerpts from the "Books of the Chronicles" (vv.21-25) /67/. This section characterises Josiah's reign, in the light of the subsequent process of history, as an episode which does no more than show how things should have been done all along; and it is followed at once by the conclusion to the account of Josiah (23:28-30).

The rest of the book concerns the destruction of the Judaean state. The sections on the kings Jehoahaz (23:31-35), Jehoiakim (23:36-24:7) and Jehoiachin (24:8-17) take us to the very end. Concerning the end itself, we have (understandably enough) no material from official sources over and above the formulaic introduction to the reign of Zedekiah (24:18) /68/. Instead, the account in 25:1-26 is obviously based on the Baruch narrative concerning the prophet Jeremiah in Jer. 39-41, except that everything to do with Jeremiah as a person is omitted; everything which does not come from Jer. 39-41 is clearly by Dtr. /69/. For example, in 25:1-12 the story of the fall of Jerusalem is, generally speaking, based on Jer. 39:1-10 except that (apart from some ornamentation in vv.2-3) Dtr. gives supplementary material on the burning of the temple in vv.8-9 /70/. However, whereas Jer. 39 moves on to the personal fate of Jeremiah, Dtr., vaguely drawing on 1 Kings 7:15ff., enumerates the pieces in the temple inventory destroyed or carried off by the Babylonians (25:13-17) and adds, presumably out of his own knowledge, something on the fate of various prominent persons in Jerusalem (25:18-21) /71/. On the other hand, he must be depending on the Baruch narrative when he inserts the section on the governor Gedaliah and his end (25:22-26). After the introductory sentence (v.22) taken from Jer. 40:7-9, vv.23-24 reproduce Jer. 40:7-9 in a shortened form and vv.25-26 briefly summarise Jer. 41. Dtr. will have intended the Gedaliah episode to show how the Judaeans who were left, by their own fault, frittered away all remaining semblance of determining their own affairs. As a conclusion, Dtr. added 25:27-30, drawn from his own knowledge. This event lacks any intrinsic historical significance but it too belongs in the account of the fate of the Judaean kings.

Section C

THE CHARACTER OF THE WORK

Chapter Ten
THE NATURE OF THE COMPOSITION

In examining the composition of the work in pp.26-74, we had
to follow the order of Dtr.'s narrative and at times deal with
fairly small points. This examination was necessary in order to
construct, or rather, restore a picture of this literary work as a
self-contained whole in spite of all the variation within it; for
anyone who looks carefully will get a clear view of the shape of
Dtr.'s work in Deuteronomy-Kings, and be able to see behind
the slight, indeed transparent, obscurity caused by the
subsequent division into individual "books", by the manifold
secondary accretions, especially at the ends of "books", and by
the later interlocking of the first section with the end of the
Pentateuchal narrative. The third and last of these
circumstances, along with the division into "books", is
principally to blame for the failure of scholars to do justice to
Dtr.'s work and to recognise it as self-standing - whereas the
Chronicler's work is automatically recognised as such, although
it is less self-contained in form and subject matter - and for the
failure to recognise Dtr.'s total independence of the Pentateuch. Yet, the interlocking of the end of the Pentateuch and
the beginning of Dtr.'s work is a simple literary development
which came about because large parts of the historical work run
parallel to each other in content, but it does not entitle us to
imagine a single original literary unit covering both Dtr. and
the Pentateuch. Rather we can see from the introduction of a
new "Deuteronomistic" stratum in Deut. 1, which goes back
over events long since treated in the Pentateuch, that the
Pentateuchal narrative, consisting of various strata but thus far
exhibiting not a trace of Dtr., suddenly gives way to a new
historical narrative. A further more general point is that the
editing of such early history fundamental to the faith - which in
the various narrative strata of the Pentateuch is based on the
combination of the sacral "Sinai tradition" and the equally

sacral "occupation tradition" /1/ - was something quite
different from writing the history of the people once they had
settled in Palestine, which had to recapitulate certain
important events of the early history only by way of
introduction. We would need very compelling reasons in order to
suppose that these two essentially different themes were
treated at the same time in one literary work or even several
literary works. There are no such reasons. It is therefore appropriate to analyse the historical narrative beginning with Deut. 1
on the basis of its own content and not to approach this analysis
with the proven findings of the literary criticism of the
Pentateuch /2/.

This does not mean that the careful analysis of
Deuteronomy-Kings which literary critics have carried out thus
far is totally wrong; on the contrary, its examination of the
structure of these books has yielded results which, generally
speaking, can be considered definitive. The analysis has gone
astray in one point only and this under the influence of the
results of Pentateuchal criticism; it has tried to explain the
structure of the written history by means of the pre-
Deuteronomistic "sources", whereas the work was not put
together until Dtr., in Deuteronomy-Kings, had adapted
material which he found in separate stories from ancient
sources. The whole purpose of examining Dtr. in detail above
was to show that it is not a matter of a "Deuteronomistic
redaction" of a historical narrative that was already more or
less complete; rather, we must say that Dtr. was the author of a
comprehensive historical work, scrupulously taking over and
quoting the existing tradition but at the same time arranging
and articulating all the material independently, and making it
clear and systematic by composing summaries which anticipate
and recapitulate. This gives the parts written by Dtr. himself a
significance quite different from what would be the case if Dtr.
were assumed to be nothing more than an editor. In these
passages we are struck by the monotonous repetition of the
same simple expressions and the continual references to divine
law, the necessity of obeying it and the disastrous consequences
of disobedience - in particular the worship of "other gods".
These passages, brought in at every suitable opportunity, which
we shall discuss below on pp.89ff., come to make good literary
sense if they are not just the monotonously repeated statement
of the pet idea of an "editor", intended to accompany and
interpret a piece of tradition already existing in finished form,

but rather meant to play a part in transforming elements totally diverse in form, scope and content, into a single literary unit. At the same time, as we showed on pp.5f. above, these comments divide a work which has grown to massive proportions into particular chronological periods. This is how we should read the long sections inserted by Dtr., especially the speeches which he wrote for the characters in his history.

Despite these elements contributed by Dtr. in order to unify the work, the separate parts of the work seem disunited and heterogeneous. The explanation is that Dtr. clearly did not intend to create something original and of a piece but was at pains to select, compile, arrange and interpret existing traditional material, which was already in written form, on the history of his people in Palestine, that is, he consciously committed himself to using the material available to him. For some periods of history this material provided not just the factual details but also the larger sequences of material - as it did for the occupation of the land west of the Jordan under Joshua or the history of the reigns of Saul and David. It is true that Dtr. needed to construct and compose by himself the account of the monarchy from Solomon onwards but here he could at least use the chronological system in the "Books of the Chronicles" to provide a solid framework. Dtr. did the largest amount of original work on the period between the occupation and the beginning of the monarchy - here he created the idea of a specific period of "judges" - though even this work is based on inference from existing traditional material (cf. above, Chapter 7). Thus, in composing the different parts of his work Dtr. was confronted with different tasks at different times; and the parts inevitably look different. However, by his construction of the work as a whole and by the sustained development of certain central ideas, Dtr. achieved that measure of unity which is so striking today. This work, if scrutinised carefully, stands out from the rest of the Old Testament as something individual and distinct from other writings. Hence our attempt to look at Dtr.'s work as the core of Deuteronomy-Kings, to trace its structure and to extract its central ideas needs no defence.

Dtr.'s work tells us virtually all we know of the history of the Israelite people in Palestine; for the Chronicler's account does no more than take fragmentary excerpts from Dtr., which it used as its source, and at most adds a little supplementary material on the history of the monarchical period which is probably derived from a different source /3/ but cannot replace

Dtr.'s work. Dtr.'s transmission of old traditional documents and accounts makes his work a most valuable historical source. Quite apart from its intrinsic value as a monument to a particular kind of theological interpretation of history and as a literary achievement, this historical value is reason enough to investigate its original constituents and its essential character.

Chapter Eleven
THE HISTORICAL PRESUPPOSITIONS

Dtr. wrote in the middle of the 6th century B.C. when the history of the Israelite people was at an end; for the later history of the post-exilic community was a completely different matter - both its internal and external conditions were different - and it was the Chronicler who first thought of explaining it as a linear continuation of the earlier history of the nation. What the historian looking back can determine about the time of Dtr., as a period of decisive change, agrees with what Dtr. quite rightly understood as symptomatic of his own age. His whole attitude is obviously shaped by the view that Israel, once settled in Palestine, slowly but surely brought upon itself its final rejection and therefore its downfall because of its repeated apostasy. Dtr. then, seeing the fall of Jerusalem, not unjustly, as the final act in a long historical drama, thought that the time had come to collect the extant traditions concerning the history of his people, to edit them into a single work and to make an interpretation of the whole which con-sidered the historical process in the light of its outcome and thus could contribute to an understanding of the situation in his own time.

With the final historical catastrophes in view, Dtr. consistently develops the idea of ever-intensifying decline throughout his work; and this is a further support for the thesis that Dtr.'s work is a unity in content and form and that it was all written at the same time, after the fall of Jerusalem /1/. He brings the idea in at the very beginning of his history. The reference to the people's lack of faith in the time of Moses, which accompanies elements of old tradition in the introductory speech by Moses (Deut. 1:22ff.) may not seem very important. However, immediately after the first section of the history proper, namely, the account of the occupation extending over only a few years in his chronological system, the theme of apostasy - beginning here and soon to intensify - is unmistakably announced in the introduction to the "judges" period (Judg. 2:11ff.), and it is diligently developed in the account of this period. Thus the emphatic and insistent warnings already issued by Moses (Deut. 4:26ff.) and Joshua

79

(Jos. 23:12ff.) in their valedictory speeches are fully justified by the subsequent course of history. According to Dtr. the moral decline reaches a sort of climax in the people's demand for a human king (1 Sam. 8:4ff.). Dtr. does, however, take the extant tradition into account by transferring the responsibility from the people to the monarchy and, at the same time, introduces the monarchy as a still unknown quantity since, after all, it was not involved in the people's ungodly demand; this enables Dtr. to join in the traditional approval of the reign of David, following the short Saul episode. He goes on from that point, however, to develop the theme of accelerating decline to the bitter end, which, as an event of the recent past, was of immediate significance to him. It was the obvious finality of this end which made him take such a serious view of the whole history of his people.

The events in Judah and Jerusalem under King Josiah, shortly before the end, are an especially important part of the historical presuppositions to Dtr.'s work. Dtr. reported this independently and in detail by giving the record of the discovery of the law (2 Kings 22:3-23:3) and including extensive excerpts from the annals regarding the king's religious measures (2 Kings 23:4-15,19-20a), and thus attributed a particular historical significance to these events. More important, these events determined his own view of the history of Israel and of what should have been the case but was not. Josiah's measures had of themselves little influence since the work of this king was nullified by his sudden death and by the impact of contemporary events of world history; rather, their influence was indirect, viz., through the work of Dtr. which in turn influenced the view of history taken in later times. Under Josiah the Deuteronomic law was found in the temple in Jerusalem /2/; and since this law was cast as a speech by Moses it was thereafter construed simply as the "law of Moses" /3/; for this reason Dtr. adopted it in the introduction to his history and so it was preserved. Thus Dtr. came to assign to the law a crucial role, regarding it as a norm for the relationship between God and people and as a yardstick by which to judge human conduct. Here we see a "legal" conception of the factors which determined the course of history - a conception which had considerable influence on Dtr.'s general attitude and which goes back to the time of Josiah as is shown by the record of the discovery of the law. It considered the whole of past history in relation to this law, concluded that the prescriptions of the law should have been observed at all times (2 Kings 22:13,17), and thus reached an unfavourable judgement on the history of Israel, seeing it as a period of disobedience to the will of God and thereby anticipating what Dtr. subsequently tried to demonstrate in detail in his account.

The events of Josiah's reign have influenced Dtr.'s conception of the Deuteronomic law in other ways as well. We must note that only particular aspects of the whole law played a practical role under Josiah and hence received attention from Dtr. Only the demand in the Deuteronomic law that there should be only one place of worship (Deut. 12:13ff.) and the various requirements directed against the continuation of Canaanite cults and rituals, that is, specifications concerned with cult, came to the forefront and had a disproportionate effect on the actions of Josiah. This may be explained by the fact that the book of the law was discovered after the cultic measures cited in 2 Kings 23:4ff. had been inaugurated. Such a treatment of the Deuteronomic law did not do justice to it as a whole. We may speculate that Josiah, who made the whole Deuteronomic law binding through a covenant (2 Kings 23:1-3), promulgated other prescriptions (of which we have no knowledge) about other parts of the law. However, the fact remains that Josiah's opportunities and constitutional powers as king were limited and did not allow him to put all the parts of the Deuteronomic law, which was not constituted as a state law /4/, into practice everywhere and without restriction, in the same way as he could act upon the prescriptions related to the law in the temple which was the official place of worship and in Jerusalem as the city belonging to David's successors /5/. The account must then be substantially correct in letting the practical influence of the Deuteronomic law extend only as far as Josiah's religious prescriptions. The historical role of the Deuteronomic law, in the period of Josiah has in fact determined the subsequent assessment of this law, especially as we see it in Dtr. Whenever Dtr. makes Moses, Joshua and others insist upon the "law", that is, the Deuteronomic law, and warn the people not to transgress it, and whenever he judges historical figures and events by the standard of the "law", he obviously means the legal ordinances concerning the worship of "other gods" and, in the case of the monarchical period especially, the legal prescription that there should be only one place of worship; he apparently ignores the rest of the law.

The way in which Dtr. describes Josiah's application of the

law makes it even more clear that he saw the "law" (the Deuteronomic law) in the light of its historical role under Josiah, i.e., in the task he ascribes to the king of carrying it out. The law itself gave no guidance on this point. The remarkable passage Deut. 17:14-20 does indeed make the law binding on the king also, but it does not tell the king what to do, on the contrary, it tries rather to restrict the traditional powers of the king as much as possible; it means by the second person singular the people as a whole, whose responsibility it is to "purge the evil from their midst" and so on /6/. In view of this it is questionable whether Josiah really acted in the spirit of the law in not only putting the law, once found, publicly into force by making a covenant, but, over and above this, in using his royal powers to guarantee the fulfilment of at least some of the prescriptions. In any case, this is what Josiah did. His actions had a direct influence on Dtr.: Dtr. elevates the events of Josiah's time to a general norm and makes it the main function of the monarchy as such to uphold the religious prescriptions in the Deuteronomic law; indeed, at the beginning of his account of the monarchy he completely departs from the intention of the law itself and transfers the responsibility for the maintenance of the relationship between God and people, as envisaged by the law, to the monarchy. This is in fact the central idea in his account of the monarchy. On one hand, then, Dtr.'s view of this part of his account is unhistorical, because he assumes that the Deuteronomic law, which is traced back to Moses, was familiar from early times and fell into oblivion only temporarily /7/. On the other hand, his view is inaccurate because he claims that the monarchy was, while it existed, responsible for the observance of the law and therefore for the preservation of the relationship between God and people. This inaccuracy is understandable, given the impression which the last, short but eventful golden age of the Davidic monarchy under Josiah made upon its contemporaries and upon the generations immediately following, an impression which gave rise to the belief attested in Dtr., that Josiah's time saw the realisation of the ideal that should have been in force throughout the monarchical period.

However, Dtr. was not too far removed from the time of the old and original order of the relationship between God and people to know that the object of his account could only be the history of the Israelite people itself. The earlier parts of his work are explicitly about this and in the second half he allows the institution of the monarchy such a prominent place simply because he felt obliged to take account of the historical significance of this phenomenon, if only because it brought about the end of the nation and because it had a momentous effect on those final developments in Dtr.'s history which determined his view of history as a whole. However, unlike the later author of the "Chronistic" work, who had only a vague idea of the original context of these phenomena, Dtr. brings the monarchy into his work in a manner designed to make clear that this institution was a late innovation, inappropriate by its nature and hence categorically objectionable, and that it accomplished a positive good only under isolated, outstanding representatives. He finds evidence in the conduct of King Josiah that the monarchy, once it existed, was responsible, in a mediatorial role, for preserving the relationship between God and people and thus, in Dtr.'s view, for observing the "law", a duty which was initially assigned to the people collectively. Therefore, the manner of Dtr.'s composition shows beyond a doubt that his main interest is always the collective history of the Israelite people; this indicates that he was still vitally close to the traditions concerning the history of the centuries before his time /8/.

Chapter Twelve

ATTITUDE TOWARDS THE MATERIAL IN THE TRADITIONS

Dtr. had no intention of fabricating the history of the Israelite people. He wished to present it objectively and base it upon the material to which he had access. Like an honest broker he began by taking, in principle, a favourable view of the material in the traditions. In describing the various historical events he spoke in his own person only at certain exceptional points, letting the old traditions speak for themselves instead. He did so even when these old traditions told of events which did not fit in with his central ideas /1/. We owe the preservation of valuable old material wholly and solely to this respect for the value of old narratives and historical accounts which reported matters of which Dtr. could have had no first-hand knowledge, to the considerable importance he placed on the traditional material and, following from it, to his reverent attitude towards historical fact /2/. Dtr. was not a redactor trying to make corrections, but a compiler of historical traditions and a narrator of the history of his people. When we have learned to regard his work as a self-contained whole, we shall find that he has crafted a work of art which merits our respect.

It is true that Dtr. did not merely assemble the traditional material used in his work; he was also selective. This is particularly demonstrable for the period of the kings of Israel and Judah. The "Books of the Chronicles" presumably contained a wealth of detailed information on this period from which Dtr. made a very restricted selection; and as we attempted to show above (p.64ff.), he by no means made an arbitrary choice of material which seemed at that moment to fit with his central ideas; but rather he selected consistently in accordance with the general approach taken in his history, drawing on the "Books of the Chronicles" for material on a few topics which he thought important and, equally consistently, omitting all other material - including the political and military activities of the kings as rulers of the state /3/ - because it did not seem essential to the treatment of his general theme. In so doing he was probably trying to write carefully and economically and to compress a long period for which there was an abundance of material (not always of special importance to him) into a relatively short account. He was not, then, slavishly dependent on the material at his disposal even though he was, generally speaking, restricted to whatever his sources had to offer.

We can be reasonably sure how Dtr. selected the material in the "Books of the Chronicles" of the kings, but no such certainty is possible with regard to the rest of his narrative because we have no idea how much material he had for the earlier periods. It is of course probable that Dtr.'s account of these periods is largely determined by the traditions still available to him and that he took these over more or less in their entirety. However, the work does show various signs of sources which Dtr. used only for particular pieces of information, without re-working them very completely, even though we cannot tell the extent and scope of these sources. Here we can disregard the whole of the introductory speech by Moses in Deut. 1-3(4) which has taken over some of the material of the old "Hexateuchal" sources; for it is only trying to provide the background for Dtr.'s own historical narrative and, furthermore, it obviously assumes a knowledge of the content of these sources /4/. On the other hand, one example of a fragment of source material, whose origin is not known, is the history found only in Dtr., of the victory of the Israelite tribes over King Og of Bashan which he regularly parallels with the victory over King Sihon of Heshbon, familiar from Num. 21. Another example is the list of Canaanite royal cities in Jos. 12:13b-24a. In particular, in 1 Sam. 7:2-8:22 and 10:17-27a /5/, Dtr. seems to have adapted material from a Samuel-Saul tradition, no longer extant: for example, details concerning the places in which Samuel was active (1 Sam. 7:16-17 /6/); the stone erected by Samuel near Mizpah (1 Sam. 7:11b-12a); the names and the activities of Samuel's sons (1 Sam. 8:2); and the designation at Mizpah of Saul as king (1 Sam. 10:21b^b-27a). These pieces of information look as though they come from the local traditions indigenous to the shrines of southern Samaria /7/. This assumption becomes more plausible if we consider that the separate stories, 1 Kings 12:32-13:32 (2 Kings 23:16-18), and 2 Kings 17:25-28 /8/, which Dtr. incorporated into his account, are local traditions from the shrine at Bethel. It appears then that Dtr. had access to various local traditions, especially those attached to the shrines of Bethel and Mizpah, both of which were situated in the same area /9/. In general, Dtr. seems to have based the account of the earlier periods on his main sources but occasionally selected those isolated elements from other traditional accounts known to him which he thought suitable to make his historical narrative complete.

Dtr.'s work nowhere refers to the words of what are known as the writing prophets. This is the more striking because in his history of the monarchical period Dtr. made heavy use of the prophetic stories which he knew, and at specific points even tells us that prophets arose (cf. 1 Kings 16:12; 2 Kings 14:25). From this we may conclude that the "Books of the Chronicles" of the kings did not mention these figures /10/ and that, in Dtr.'s time, collections of their prophecies did not yet exist.

Dtr. not only assembled and selected his material but also linked the various traditions at his disposal and tried to eliminate inconsistencies between them because he wanted to construct a complete self-contained work. Since he valued all his sources equally as historical documents and it therefore did not occur to him to examine them critically, he had simply to add together the information at his disposal and, as a result, he used one source to supply what appeared to be lacking in another. The most obvious example of this is his account of the "judges" period. Here Dtr. inferred from the fact that Jephthah appeared in both of his main sources - the series of heroic stories and the catalogue of "(minor) judges" - that, generally speaking, his sources could simply be added together, and out of this addition he created the picture of the warrior-"judges", incumbents of a clearly defined office who did not succeed each other without a break but appeared soon after one another; and finally he treated Samuel, who traditionally came at the end of the premonarchical period, as one of these. Similarly, in his account of the occupation, Dtr. has created a clear and simple pattern by combining the various source materials at his disposal; he attaches the story of the victory over King Og of Bashan, which he picked up somewhere, to the Sihon story and thereby sets up a parallel between the story of the occupation, according to plan, of what was to be the Israelites' share of Transjordanian land under Moses and the story of the conquest of the land west of the Jordan, which is a familiar part of the tradition of the occupation found in Joshua. Dtr. was motivated by the universal human inclination to see the historical process, as relatively clear and simple in its movement /11/, and so he endeavoured to find in the various separate traditions, large and small, to which he had access a simple historical process, and to depict it in the sections of his work, which was meant to be as self-contained and homogeneous as possible. This he does by simple addition and, at times, by giving particular details from the tradition a more general application.

Admittedly he occasionally had to try to reconcile conflicting information from his various sources or else fill in gaps. In Deut. 27:*2ff. Moses stipulated that an altar be built on Mount Ebal after the crossing of the Jordan /12/; Dtr. regarded the failure of the occupation tradition to tell us that this was accordingly done as a purely accidental gap and so he himself incorporated the missing information at what seemed to be an appropriate point (Jos. 8:*30-35). In a prophecy David was forbidden to build the temple as planned (2 Sam. 7:1ff.) but, according to the tradition, Solomon undertook to build the temple because this work was pleasing to God. Dtr. decided that the categorical prohibition could be taken to be merely temporary and so he added to Nathan's prophecy to David a reference to Solomon as the future builder of the temple (2 Sam. 7:13a); then, in the long section on the building of the temple which is Dtr.'s own work, he interpreted this temporary prohibition to mean that it was because of that the wars which David had to fight to consolidate his state he could not build the temple (1 Kings 5:17). Thus Dtr. has found a simple though not quite inaccurate way to resolve a discrepancy between the accounts known to him, for his own favourable opinion of the temple made it impossible for him to follow the real sense of the prophecy in 2 Sam. 7:1-7 and declare that Solomon went against the will of God when he built the temple.

Finally Dtr. has occasionally corrected the traditions he has utilised. These corrections are mostly unintentional but unmistakable. For by linking the different traditions and integrating them into the whole design of his history in the way he did, he often gave them a meaning and significance at variance with the material really contained in them. Therefore we cannot simply reconstruct the history of Israel on the basis of Dtr.'s account; rather one must disentangle the original separate complexes of tradition from the pattern imposed upon them by Dtr. and investigate them in isolation in order to discover their bases and their subject-matter. Dtr. has given his sources a content in part alien to their original character and thus made them look quite different; above all in the occupation story, where he juxtaposes the section on Transjordan with the section on the land west of the Jordan, and in the "judges" narrative, where he combines materials from separate traditions Dtr.

proceeds as he does out of the simple conviction that he is accurately interpreting the traditions by comparing them with each other. It is only in the story of Saul's accession that Dtr. made a conscious correction /13/, that is, an alteration of the evident sense of the source used which is not motivated in any other tradition; and here he is interested not so much in the course of events as such but in how to evaluate it. Elsewhere he has respected his sources so highly that he has put them into his account without deletion; he did no more than append long comments in which he is visibly struggling to show the tradition in what he thinks is the proper light. We can make sense of Dtr.'s one very exceptional contradiction of the account given by his source only if we consider that the passage is concerned to judge the institution of monarchy which thereafter stands in the foreground of Dtr.'s history - hence this moment in history is particularly important to Dtr. Moreover Dtr. was quite confident about his verdict on the monarchy; for him it followed naturally from the history and the downfall of the monarchy and besides was clearly implied in the Deuteronomic law which went back to Moses (Deut. 17:14-20). Dtr. did take over the entire text of his source concerning Saul's accession and, together with the supplementary material which he added, this made for a very disconnected narrative, as he surely realised himself; in particular, the matter of the decisive Philistine victory is full of contradictions. All this goes to show Dtr.'s commitment to the traditions which came and serves to confirm that he follows his sources in a conscientious manner noticeable everywhere. The case we have mentioned is unique and this explains why Dtr. departed here from his normal practice /14/ and used his own words not only to summarise and interpret but also, in places, to narrate.

In general, then, Dtr. gave his narrative very markedly the character of a traditional work, the intention was to be a compilation and explanation of the extant traditions concerning the history of his people.

Chapter Thirteen

THE CENTRAL THEOLOGICAL IDEAS

Dtr. did not write his history to provide entertainment in hours of leisure or to satisfy a curiosity about national history, but intended it to teach the true meaning of the history of Israel from the occupation to the destruction of the old order. The meaning which he discovered was that God was recognisably at work in this history, continuously meeting the accelerating moral decline with warnings and punishments and, finally, when these proved fruitless, with total annihilation. Dtr., then, perceives a just divine retribution in the history of the people, though not so much (as yet) in the fate of the individual. He sees this as the great unifying factor in the course of events, and speaks of it not in general terms but in relation to the countless specific details reported in the extant traditions. Thus Dtr. approached his work with a definite theological conviction. He certainly does not think that the history of the Israelite people is a mere random example of the fate of peoples whose end is at hand but rather regards it as a unique case, quite apart from the fact that the people concerned are his own people. Dtr. gives various hints that God honoured the Israelite people with a special role and thus placed them under a special obligation, which was formulated in the Deuteronomic law which Dtr. places at the beginning of his history; this law was essentially intended to keep them from forsaking God in any way, that is, to demand an exclusive bond with the one God and thereby to assure the worship of one particular God - an exclusiveness unique in the history of ancient religion. The very fact that Dtr. repeatedly mentions apostasy, although he uses no specific technical term for it, shows that he seeks not to describe just any collective fate, but to portray the development of a nation living under particular conditions.

In this task, Dtr. focuses his attention upon specific theological presuppositions to which he alludes only occasionally in his narrative and which he does not articulate or expound as a whole; clearly, he expects the reader to be familiar with them. His interest centres on the special bond between God and people to which he refers when, with the old traditions (1 Sam. 9:16; 2 Sam. 7:7f., etc.) in mind, he speaks of Israel as "God's people" (1 Sam. 12:22; 1 Kings 8:16; 16:2, etc.; cf. also 1 Kings 8:53). He did find the extremely unusual concept of a "chosen people" in the Deuteronomic law (Deut. 14:2) and its framework (Deut. 7:6), but does not himself use it to characterise the position of the people of Israel. However it seems that, following tradition, he liked to describe the relationship between God and people as a "covenant"; here he did not have in mind the act of making a covenant in its original sense but rather the permanent regulation, as defined in the law, of the relationship between God and people. This is shown by his independent use of the term "ark of the covenant of Yahweh" to describe the ark and his habit of incorporating this term into his source material instead of using the older expression "ark of Yahweh". Moreover, in Deut. 9:9ff. he equates the concepts of "covenant" and "law" (cf. Deut 4:13), and in Deut. 10:1ff. regards the stone tablets which contain the basic law, the decalogue, as the contents of the ark (cf. 1 Kings 8:9,21). Thus in his view the special relationship between God and people is confirmed through the promulgation of the law, of which the Deuteronomic law is, according to Deut. 5:28ff., the authentic divine exposition. This relationship is therefore - here he merely follows the old tradition - confirmed once in history by the theophany on the mountain of God to which he gives the name Horeb (Deut. 4:10ff.) and it is associated with miraculous manifestations of divine powers to which Dtr. alludes as a matter of general knowledge in his frequent references to "being brought up out of Egypt". Among these manifestations - and here Dtr. follows the content of the old "occupation tradition" (von Rad) - is the conquest of the "good" land of Palestine (Deut. 1:35, etc.) which was already promised to the ancestors, and described by Dtr. on the basis of detailed accounts in the sources; this conquest succeeded because God "was with Moses and Joshua" (Deut. 31:8; Jos 1:5,17; 3:7) and shaped the course of events. Further examples so ordered of how Dtr. saw divine intervention in history are seen, for example, where the kings whose territory has been promised to the Israelite tribes stubbornly resist their passage (cf. Deut. 2:26ff.) and so bring about their own elimination.

Of the events from the sphere of the "Sinai tradition" which are of fundamental importance for the relationship between God and people, Dtr. has, then, mentioned only - and that briefly - the theophany on Horeb and the promulgation of the decalogue, going into detail only when he gives the whole Deuteronomic law with connecting passages by way of exposition of the decalogue. From the sphere of the "occupation tradition" /1/ he occasionally refers in passing to the promise of the land to the Israelites' ancestors and the bringing up from Egypt and then, following a summary of the period of the wanderings in the wilderness, he describes the conquest of Palestine in detail because he had a specific source at hand. All these things prepared the way for the real theme of his history, the conduct and fate of the people once they had settled in Palestine. Dtr. constructed his history as he did in order to show that the early events committed the people to unbroken loyalty to God as manifested in observance of the law, the more so because (as Dtr. says in 1 Kings 8:23, in connection with Deut. 7:9,12) this God "keeps covenant and steadfast love" and is, moreover, a just judge who passes the right sentence not only on individuals (1 Kings 8:31f.) but also on the people as a whole, even if he waits patiently and in the "judges" period gives the people one "saviour" after another despite their unfaithfulness and, what is more, meets the people's demand for a king, recognises the king as his "anointed" (1 Sam. 12:3,5) and gives the monarchy a chance to prove itself beneficial to the people (1 Sam. 12:20ff.) in their subsequent history. For Dtr. then the demand for observance of the divine law has as its background the fact that God has manifested himself and acted at the beginning of Israelite history and has repeatedly intervened to help.

Although in this traditional history of the Israelite people Dtr. has little chance to mention that God's actions were intended to have an effect on the whole world, he does so once, in 1 Kings 8:41-43, where he makes "foreigners", that is, members of other races, pray to the God of Israel who "causes his name to dwell" in the temple of Jerusalem and then goes so far as to make it an ideal to be realised in the future that one day "all the peoples of the earth" will "learn to know and fear" this God (cf. 8:60). In similar fashion the prophet Ezekiel, roughly contemporary with Dtr., speaks of the purpose of God's action. Similarly Dtr. presents the history of Israel as a preparation for greater things. However, this idea does not take on any significance for Dtr.; in his casual statement of it he is merely imitating a manner of speaking popular in his time. In general he saw the history of Israel as a self-contained process which began with specific manifestations of power and came to a definitive end with the destruction of Jerusalem.

In keeping with all his presuppositions Dtr. has centred his history on the theme of worship of God as required by the law, or defined in a strict, rather narrow sense; for he is interested not so much in the development of possible forms of worship of God as in the various possible forms of deviation from this worship which could be construed as apostasy and how these were realised in history. Hence, the law is needed not in a positive role to prescribe the forms of worship, which were indicated by current religious practice throughout the ancient Near East, but rather to prohibit the forms of worship which were wrong; this was in fact one of Dtr.'s main concerns. According to Dtr., the law itself was stated in its essentials in the decalogue; since, according to Deut. 10:1ff., the stone tablets on which the original text of the decalogue had been inscribed were deposited in the "ark of the covenant of Yahweh", the ark took on a central importance for Dtr. On one hand, then, he saw the decalogue on the stone tablets as the original form of God's law, withheld from the gaze of the profane, concealed and guarded by cultic officials. On the other hand, the document of practical significance was the Deuteronomic law, the authentic exposition of the decalogue; and he means the Deuteronomic law, when he speaks of "the law (of Moses)", when he requires it to be read out regularly (Deut. 31:10ff.) and reports that Joshua obeyed this requirement (Jos. 8:34), or when he refers to the law in the course of general admonitions (Jos. 23:6; 1 Kings 2:3; 2 Kings 10:31; 17:13), or when he speaks of the observance of some particular clause of the law (Jos. 8:31; 2 Kings 14:6; 23:21). In each of these instances we can prove that Dtr. is alluding to the Deuteronomic law. Thinking of the application of the Deuteronomic law under Josiah, he pays particular and disproportionate attention to the religious prescriptions contained in the law (cf. above, pp.81f.) and these prescriptions have considerable influence on his view of cult and of the general nature of men's worship of God.

Because Dtr. takes so much notice of the cultic prescriptions in the Deuteronomic law, he adopts a strongly negative attitude toward particular aspects of cult; and since, out of all the regulations on worship contained in the law, he gives special, one-sided attention to matters of cult, he forms a generally pessimistic view of the possibilities of men's worship. In taking this view he has correctly understood the attitude of the Deuteronomic law to cultic activities; for, apart from the fact that the commandment to have a single place of worship implies that the practice of cult must be drastically reduced, the law shows a distinct lack of interest in the observance of cult and is interested instead in preventing all manner of cults and cult practices which it thinks illegitimate. Similarly there is no sign that Dtr. was actively interested in the performance of cult activities and he likes to confer upon cult objects and institutions a significance not strictly speaking cultic, as well as indicating their original and actual function. He does not ignore an activity of cult sanctioned by the Deuteronomic law or deny that it was authorised but he attaches no special importance to it. For example, he sees the ark in its role as the "ark of the covenant of Yahweh" principally as the repository of the autograph of the fundamentally important decalogue. Naturally he was well aware of its original cultic significance and recognises this by introducing the (levitical) priests as bearers of the ark (Jos. 3-4, Jos. 6 and 1 Kings 8:1-13), thereby entrusting this sacred object to certain persons who had the exclusive right to perform cult activities. However, he never relates the ark directly to cultic practices, not even in Jos. 8:*30-35, which he added himself; here he explicitly mentions the presence of the ark among the Israelite tribes, which seems appropriate, given Jos. 3-4 and 6, but he mentions it, not as part of the preliminaries of sacrifice, but only just before the subsequent reading of the law.

It is even more remarkable that Dtr. is not interested in cult proper as part of his conception of the significance of the temple in Jerusalem as described in Solomon's prayer of dedication (1 Kings 8:14-53). In 1 Kings 8:5 Dtr. does follow his source in saying that the bringing of the ark to the temple was accompanied with great sacrifices, and in his own addition (1 Kings 8:62ff.) he tells of abundant sacrifices following the prayer of dedication /2/. This he thought self-evident and legitimate. He accepts, then, that sacrifice was inevitably a customary form of worship, provided that it took a form authorised by the Deuteronomic law, but he gives it such a peripheral importance that Solomon's prayer of dedication says nothing whatsoever on the role of the temple as a place of sacrifice, even though Dtr. must surely have known that this was originally its main practical function. Dtr. took over the formula in the Deuteronomic law which describes the temple as the "dwelling" "chosen" by God for his "name". However, whereas the Deuteronomic law had used this formula to justify

93

the recognition of the temple as a legitimate place of sacrifice
(cf. Deut. 12:13f. and passim), Dtr. surpassed the Deuteronomic
law in devaluing cultic sacrifice and completely disregarding
sacrifice altogether, and so formulated his own conception of
the significance of the temple. For him the temple is little
more than a place towards which one turns in prayer, the
location of the invisible divine presence - this is more or less
what is meant by "the dwelling place of God's name" in this
place - which determines the direction in which one should
pray, the Kibla /3/. The only other function attributed to the
temple is in vv.31f., that of the place of divine judgements,
which are responsible for determining the verdict related to the
administration of justice in particular, prescribed cases. In this
passage, allusions to sacrifice are conspicuous by their absence,
the more so because the formal religious occasions mentioned
in Solomon's prayer of dedication were normally accompanied
by supplicatory sacrifices. One can be sure that Dtr. has in
mind the situation in his own time, when the temple had been
destroyed and a sacrificial cult on the usual scale was therefore
no longer practicable in Jerusalem, but the prayers of those
who remained in the land and of those who had been deported
probably were directed towards the site of the old temple, in
memory of the past, although they could no longer be supported
by supplicatory sacrifice /4/. This is certainly what happened;
but it is still curious that Dtr. knew perfectly well that the
temple used to be a centre of regular sacrifices, and, although
he did not regard other aspects of his own time as normal, but
saw in his own time the end of the history of his people, he even
so did not see the end of regulated cult as any great loss. Thus
he lets Solomon describe the significance of the temple which
he has just built without so much as mentioning sacrifice. In
this Dtr. is in direct succession to the Deuteronomic law. His
concern with the temple as the place of sacrifice is purely
negative; he expresses this not in the prayer of dedication but in
comments which recur throughout his account of the subsequent
history of the monarchy. Here he follows the assertion in the
Deuteronomic law that the temple is the one legitimate centre
for cult at such times as it may be appropriate to perform
sacrifices. Dtr. found such sacrifices acceptable, provided that
they took a legitimate form, but did not lay any stress upon
them. On the positive side, however, in the long prayer of
dedication Dtr. characterises the erection of the temple as an
historical milestone and goes on to extract from the "Books of

the Chronicles of the Kings of Judah" any material relevant to the temple. The value which the temple of Jerusalem had for him is entirely based on its actual historical role, which he explained - drawing upon the Deuteronomic law - as the "dwelling place for Yahweh's name" in Jerusalem, the city "chosen" by Yahweh for this purpose (cf. 1 Kings 11:13,32,34,36; 14:21; 2 Kings 21:7; 23:27); further, he adduces the fact that it was the repository of the holy ark with the tablets of the law (cf. 1 Kings 8:9,21), and finally, the fact that it was, in accordance with the Deuteronomic law, the one and only legitimate centre of the cult, so long as cultic sacrifice was carried out.

We cannot tell how Dtr. thought that the Deuteronomic requirement that there be only one place of worship had been met in the time before Solomon built the temple; for he assumes that the law was familiar from the time of Moses onward, and must therefore have taken for granted that even in earlier times some temporary provision was made to meet what he considers the most important requirement of the law. However, he has said nothing definite about the matter. In fact, he has simply reported all manner of sacrifices found in his old sources without censuring them on the ground of this stipulation of a single place of worship. He probably allowed the law to be interpreted fairly loosely in this temporary situation. Jos. 8:*30-35, which he inserted himself, reports the sacrifice authorised by the command of Moses in Deut. 27:2ff. and then mentions the presence of the ark. Even though this is not supported by Deut. 27 and the ark is not connected explicitly with the sacrifice, it suggests that Dtr. might consider sacrifice with the ark at hand to be justified; this would make the sacrifice in Shiloh legitimate (1 Sam. 1:3ff.; 2:12ff.). Gideon's sacrifice (Judg. 6:11-24) was, of course, explained adequately by the appearance of God's messenger or God himself /5/; the same is true of Solomon's sacrifice in Gibeon. Elsewhere Dtr. tacitly uses the presence of a "man of God" or the like as a justification for sacrifices performed outside Jerusalem before the completion of the Jerusalem temple; this would apply to the sacrifice at the "high place" of an unknown city in the presence of Samuel (1 Sam. 9:12ff.) and even to Elijah's sacrifice on Mount Carmel (1 Kings 18:30ff.) /6/. Dtr. probably based this view upon 1 Sam. 10:8 and 13:7b-14 - the secondary part of the old Saul tradition which, however, had formed a part of Dtr.'s source. Here it was a sin for Saul to perform a sacrifice without

95

waiting for Samuel. Dtr. also dealt with Samuel's sacrifices in parts of the history composed by himself - for example the account of the great assembly in Mizpah (1 Sam. 7:9f.), and the report that Samuel built an altar in Ramah (1 Sam. 7:17). On the other hand, Dtr. probably did not regard the activity in 1 Sam. 14:33-35 as a sacrifice, since sacrifice is not explicitly mentioned here, but probably saw it as a "profane slaughter" in the sense of Deut. 12:20ff., even though the incident was originally understood to be a sacrifice, as is shown by the reference to the altar in v.35. In general, however, Dtr. seems to have kept as close as possible to his sources, even in a matter of such importance to him, without altering or even adding comments to them. This is in keeping with his basically favourable opinion regarding the traditions to which he had access. In accordance with this he was apparently relatively lenient about the sacrifices made in the different cult centres in Israel before the time of Solomon, finding some way to justify such practices and not interpreting the stipulation of a single place of worship as strictly as the Deuteronomic law sets it out, until the Jerusalem temple was built. This is a further proof that Dtr. did not intend to write his history to fit a pre-determined theory but took the tradition into account and somewhat modified any strictness of theory. Tradition gave a favourable picture of Samuel; therefore, because of his division of history into periods, Dtr. saw reason to include Samuel in the series of "judges" to whom he is consistently favourably disposed. This means that he does not criticise, on the basis of the Deuteronomic law, the sacrifices which the traditions report that Samuel offered, in the way that he later criticises sacrifices offered by the kings of Israel and Judah, whom he tends to view negatively. Instead, in his discussion of Samuel's action, he interprets the stipulation in the Deuteronomic law that there should be only one place of worship as if it were not strictly binding before the time of Solomon. He judges other instances in the same manner. It appears to be the tradition about Samuel, however, which matters to him whenever he inquires into the application of the regulation about the single place of worship prior to Solomon. Thus in his account of the period before the Jerusalem temple was built, Dtr. uses only the highly generalised Deuteronomic warning against worshipping other gods as a criterion by which to judge historical events and characters. We see this in the way he adapts the history of the "judges". It is only with Solomon that he begins to make sacrifices on "high places" outside Jerusalem the main transgression against the law, in his critical examination of the history which he is describing.

Finally we must raise the question of what historical developments Dtr. anticipated for the future. Admittedly his theme is the past history of his people, as written down and, as far as he was concerned, at an end. However, the pre-exilic prophets saw the catastrophe which they predicted not as a final end but as the beginning of a new era. Similarly, Dtr. could have seen the end of the period of history which he depicts as the end of a self-contained historical process, without thinking that his people could go no further; and he could have used the interpretative summaries, which he adds, to answer the question that readily suggests itself: would not the history which he wrote attain its full meaning in the future, in conditions which had yet to develop out of the ruins of the old order, the more so because in Dtr.'s time people were intensely hopeful that a new order of things would emerge from all these catastrophes? It is very telling that Dtr. does not take up this question and does not use the opportunity to discuss the future goal of history. Clearly he saw the divine judgement which was acted out in his account of the external collapse of Israel as a nation as something final and definitive and he expressed no hope for the future, not even in the very modest and simple form of an expectation that the deported and dispersed people would be gathered together. On one hand, it was appropriate to threaten deportation as the final divine punishment for disobedience, as Dtr. emphasises in the introductory speech by Moses in Deut. 4:25-28 and then more briefly and at times only allusively in Joshua's speech in Jos. 23:15b-16 and in Samuel's speech in 1 Sam. 12:25. On the other hand, there was every reason to speak of the more distant future in connection with reflection on the past destruction of the northern kingdom and on the future destruction of the state of Judah in 2 Kings 17:7ff. and 21:12ff. or in a final remark at the end of the whole work. The most unambiguous information on this point is to be had in the last part of Solomon's prayer of dedication (1 Kings 8:44-53). At this early stage Dtr. makes Solomon look at the possibility of future dispersion but he is thinking only that the prayers of the dispersed people would then be directed towards the site of the Jerusalem temple; he makes Solomon wish that these prayers be heard but he makes the prayers contain nothing but a petition for forgiveness of past guilt without even

97

suggesting that the nation might later be re-assembled and reconstructed. Under these circumstances Dtr. cannot mean the improvement in the deported Jehoiachin's personal fortunes (2 Kings 25:27-30) to herald a new age. Apart from the fact that the subject matter of this event does not lend itself to such a comprehensive interpretation, in view of what we have said above, Dtr. would have no reason to take such a view. On the contrary, he shows his usual scrupulous respect for historical fact in reporting the last information that he has about the history of the Judaean monarchy as a simple fact.

On this matter, then, Dtr.'s theological outlook corresponds to that of the Deuteronomic law most closely. In the light of conditions in its own time, the Deuteronomic law sees nothing but the order of things given and willed by God in the time of Moses, without ever considering an historical purpose outside this present situation /7/. Similarly, the possibility of the destruction of the people, already envisaged by the Deuteronomic law as punishment for disobedience, was now for Dtr. an accomplished historical reality. Thus he thought that the order of things as put forward in the Deuteronomic law had reached a final end, an end which his whole history is intent upon explaining as a divine judgement. The close relationship of the Deuteronomic law to the contemporary situation because of intervening historical events, was the cause of Dtr.'s concentration upon the past. Dtr. clearly knew nothing about the additions to the Deuteronomic law which postulate a new future /8/. In any case, his interpretation of the facts and, probably, the time in which he wrote, are far closer to those of the original Deuteronomic law than to those of the author of the secondary passages /9/.

Not even the occasional reference to God's intention to deal with all peoples by his activity causes Dtr. to look at the future; here too he does not go beyond the situation of his own time. This is strange, as the prophets who are closest to him chronologically, Deutero-Isaiah (Is. 52:10) and Ezekiel (Ezek. 36:36 and passim), endow God's future actions with the goal that "all peoples" should see them and should come to recognise God. Dtr. did use this last statement but did not relate the nations" knowledge of God to great events of the future but to present and visible circumstances, even if this knowledge of God would take some time to arise and grow in them; here he has in mind the existence of the holy place in Jerusalem with which "the great name of God" and the contemplation of God's great deeds in the past are associated (1 Kings 8:41-43), the answering of Israel's prayers which God receives in this holy place (1 Kings 8:60) and finally the divine judgement pronounced on people and sanctuary which will make "all peoples" attend to the judging God (1 Kings 9:7-9). Here again Dtr. is interested exclusively in the past and present.

All this at least tells us what Dtr.'s spiritual world is not. His work is not of an official nature, nor did it come from the priestly sphere - we have demonstrated his significant lack of interest in cult - nor is it rooted in the attitude of the governing class, for his censure of the monarchy as an institution and his description of it as a secondary phenomenon in the history of the nation are crucial to his approach to history. The view that the great final catastrophes were a divine judgement towards which the Israelite people were precipitated in the course of their history is in the spirit of the "writing" prophets, but this spirit is not a determining factor in Dtr.'s work, as we see from the complete absence of projection into the future. This fact also rules out the possibility that Dtr. followed the ideology of the so-called national prophets. The negative characteristics of Dtr. are exactly the same as those in the Deuteronomic law. Furthermore, there is no evidence that Dtr. was commissioned by an individual or by a particular group. Hence the history was probably the independent project of a man whom the historical catastrophes he witnessed had inspired with curiosity about the meaning of what had happened, and who tried to answer this question in a comprehensive and self-contained historical account, using those traditions concerning the history of his people to which he had access /10/.

Notes to Chapter One
THE TASK BEFORE US

1   In general, von Rad's Das formgeschichtliche Problem des Hexateuchs (1938 [ET 1966]) has reached most decisive results concerning the essence and development of the Pentateuch.

2   In passing, it will be necessary to discuss certain details about the growth of the Pentateuch which bear upon our analysis of the Deuteronomistic work.

3   We cannot go into the problem at this point of whether the Deuteronomistic work is something completely new in the whole sphere of ancient Near Eastern literature. However, one can nonetheless assess its significance in accordance with this fact. In any case, one could find precursors to the Deuteronomist within the Old Testament; the Yahwist would be the prime example (on whose nature and work, cf. von Rad [1938], pp.46ff. [ET 1966: 50ff.]). The most important and, for our purposes, most essential difference between them lies in the fact that the main contents and the structure of the individual parts of the Yahwistic work were already provided by traditions originally rooted in the cult; on the other hand, the author of the Deuteronomistic work had to order the disposition of the whole material himself on the basis of the material available to him; for that only certain sections of the historical process he wished to describe were already in existence in the form of connected traditions.

Notes to Chapter Two
EVIDENCE THAT THE WORK IS A SELF-CONTAINED WHOLE

1   For reasons which I shall explain later I avoid the usual symbol D which is based on the customary practice of designating the different literary strata in the "Hexateuch" with a single capital letter. To avoid misunderstanding, I shall reserve the abbreviation Dt. [Translator's note: "Dt" has been replaced in the translation by "the Deuteronomic law"] for the Deuteronomic law and its framework. The abbreviation Deut.,

followed by chapter and verse numbers, is used for the present book of Deuteronomy, the "fifth book of Moses".

2   At one time (Noth 1938a: XIV,7) I left open the possibility that Jos. 1:12ff. was interpolated by a later hand into Dtr.'s work. But this should probably be rejected since there are no solid reasons for it.

3   The old view that 1 Sam. 12 is "Deuteronomistic" (cf. Wellhausen 1899: 243; Kuenen 1890: 46, n.6) is absolutely right. The language of this chapter, especially in vv.9,10,14,15,20,24, is undoubtedly "Deuteronomistic". 1 Sam. 12 is commonly attributed to an older "theocratic" narrative "source" (E) already similar in many ways to Dtr. (cf. Eissfeldt 1934: 307 [ET 1965: 272]; also Weiser 1939: 13 [ET 1965: 272]). But this is based not on a new, improved analysis of the actual chapter but on generalised literary-critical presuppositions which I cannot think are correct. See below pp.51f.

4   See below pp.93ff.

5   E.g. Eissfeldt 1934: 285f., (301), (316f.), 337ff. [cf. ET 1965: 242ff., 246f., 255f., 266f., 280f., 299ff.]

6   E.g. substantial parts of Solomon's prayer of dedication (1 Kings 8:14ff.) are attributed to a "second redactor" by Eissfeldt 1934: 339 [ET 1965: 301].

7   Rudolph 1938: 240-44.

8   Rudolph rightly deletes the obvious glosses Judg. 2:17 and 3:1b,2. But his neglect of the whole of Jos. 24 in his investigation of the literary growth of the complex of traditions Jos. 23:1 - Judg. 3:6, cannot be justified and shows that he is anticipating the result for which he is aiming - viz. that everything else is "Deuteronomistic".

9   The necessity of transferring Judg. 2:23 and 3:5 from their traditional place to somewhere quite different shows that everything is not quite straightforward here.

10   Which of the three sentences constitutes the original text, we cannot and need not decide.

11   The introductory words literally repeat those in v.14; the latter are motivated by what precedes them but the former have no such connection since the following verses go back before the time of the preceding verses. One can connect them directly with one of the variants in vv.11b,12,13 (so Rudolph et al.), but one can just as well regard them as a phrase taken from the earlier passage to introduce a more extensive addition.

12   Rudolph 1938: 242 rightly sees Judg. 3:3 as "a brief summary of Jos. 13:2b-6a". But this Joshua section is not only

part of the addition to Dtr.'s account in Jos. 13ff. (see below pp.40f.) but also belongs to the secondary elements within this addition (cf. Noth 1938a: 46f.). This means that we cannot adopt Rudolph's view that Judg. 3:3 belongs to the original "Deuteronomistic redaction" of Joshua.

13   In Judg. 2:23 the verbs could be translated as pluperfect. Then the verse need not conflict with v.21b. But it could easily have been added following the addition of v.22. On Judg. 3:1b,2, cf. above, n.8.

14   Rudolph was right to emphasise that Judg. 2:6 is directly and closely linked to Jos. 23 (Rudolph 1938: 241). Within the straightforward context of Judg. 2:6-10 the statements on Joshua's age and his burial place should also be attributed to Dtr. Since Dtr. is capable of making similar statements, e.g., about the "minor judges" in Judges (see below, pp.42f.), we are not entitled to attribute Judg. 2:8-9 to a "source" preserved in the Old Testament. On literary-critical grounds we must assume that this information was taken over by a secondary hand from Judg. 2 into Jos. 24:29-31 when the book of Joshua was made into an independent literary unit and thus a concluding remark on the death of Joshua was felt to be necessary. In this process Judg. 2:7 (= Jos. 24:31) was put in after Judg. 2:8-9 (= Jos. 24:29-30), losing the appropriate order of Judg. 2, in order to give the book an resounding ending. Later the statement in Jos. 24:32, compiled from other Old Testament passages (cf. Noth 1938a: 110), and finally Jos. 24:33 were added.

15   It is generally assumed that Dtr. composed Jos. 23 using Jos. 24 as his model. I used to share this assumption (1938a: 101) but it is in reality unfounded. The correspondences are of a general nature and consist merely in the following: Joshua calls a meeting of the Israelite tribes, makes a speech and in this speech recollects the past and tells them how to conduct themselves in the future. This is so typical of Dtr., who often inserts speeches by historical characters, that we have no reason to suppose that his model here was Jos. 24. Even less probable is the generally held belief that Jos. 24 was once part of the pre-Deuteronomistic occupation tradition but was omitted by Dtr. because he took exception to certain parts of it - in such matters he is not nearly so petty as is commonly believed (cf. below pp.84f.) - and replaced by Jos. 23 to be later put in again after Jos. 23. The alternative to this thoroughly contrived view is obtained by reconstructing the literary process as follows. The passage Jos. 24:1-28 which stands by

itself and has an independent origin (cf. Noth 1938a: 108f.) shows no knowledge of the traditional version of the conquest in Jos. 2ff., and this passage was apparently unknown to Dtr. It was subsequently revised extensively in the style of Dtr. (cf. Noth 1938a: 105f.) and incorporated into Dtr.'s long historical composition at a suitable point, because it contributes something important to the history of Joshua. Later the secondary verses 29-33 were added (cf. n.14 above).

16   The fragmentary nature of Judg. 1 is conspicuous throughout - in the strangely abrupt introduction of Adoni-bezek in v.5, in the unmotivated appearance of Jerusalem in v.7, in the confusion between Judah and Kaleb in vv.10ff., in the isolated position of the statements in v.16, and in the unresolved contradiction between v.18 and v.19, etc. This obviously cannot be explained away by text-critical emendations.

17   For further details see Noth 1938a: XIf.,3ff.,19ff.,29ff.

18   Scholars are right to see in both Judges and Kings a "Deuteronomistic framework" which encompasses the old traditional material. The attribution of the connecting elements to still older "sources" or simply to "E" is based not on new results of literary-critical analysis but on general literary-critical assumptions (cf., e.g., Eissfeldt 1934: 293ff. [ET 1965: 244ff.]).

19   In principle, it is immaterial whether one identifies these sources with the "Hexateuchal" sources or only sees them as analogous.

20   It is only in the case of 1 and 2 Kings that the circumstances forced scholars to conclude that the traditional material was not, at least in the main, originally compiled by a "Deuteronomistic editor".

21   As Dtr. himself continually notes, for the history of the kings he made a selection from the official documents available to him. For the plan behind this selection, cf. below, pp.64ff.

Notes to Chapter Three
THE BEGINNING OF THE HISTORY

1   Cf. Hempel 1930: 82; Sellin 1933: 80f. (ET 1923: 124f.); et al. Little attempt has been made to ascertain the total extent of the Deuteronomistic work.

2   Quite rightly, no one has yet, as far as I know,

interpreted the occasional passages where the old text is augmented in Deuteronomistic style, e.g. Ex. 23:20ff. and Ex. 34:10ff., as a sign of a thorough "redaction". Num. 21:33-35 is a secondary addition, taken word for word from Deut. 3:1-3.

3   For further details of the re-working of the history of Saul and David, see below pp.54ff.

4   Deut. 4:41-43 is certainly a later addition made up of Deut. 19:2a,3b,4,5b and Jos. 20:8. Deut. 4:1-40 has from the start a different tone and its subject matter distinguishes it from Deut. 1-3. For the significance of this passage in its present setting, cf. below pp.33f.

5   For details on the relationship of Deut. 1-3 to the passages treating the same events in Numbers, cf. below pp.26ff. Even a superficial examination will show us that Deut. 1-3 is not a mere slavish rendering of materials found elsewhere

6   Admittedly this chapter has been much expanded, possibly by a later hand - cf. below p.31.

7   On the close correspondence - especially in language and style - between Jos. 14:6-14 and Deut. 1, cf. Noth 1938a: 57.

8   It is possible that Dtr.'s inclination to insert speeches is dependent on the extant form of the Deuteronomic law or at least influenced by it.

9   Hölscher 1922: 176ff.

10   E.g., Eissfeldt 1934: 266 [ET 1965: 225].

11   I am not concerned here to explain individual verses but discuss only the larger complexes.

12   9:22-24 is an addition which is relevant to the content but which disturbs the connection. The ark has already been mentioned (vv.8-9) in 10:1ff., where it is for the first time described as the receptacle for the tables of the law; but the statement at the end of this long interpolation about the Levites, service for the ark is just as surely an addition as is the fragment of itinerary in vv.6-7, the source of which is unknown but which was read in Deut. 10 and used by the editor of Num. 33:30b-34a (cf. Noth 1940a: 20 n.1).

Notes to Chapter Four
THE CHRONOLOGICAL FRAMEWORK

1   This is based above all on the significance which the Deuteronomic law has for him: cf. below pp.93ff.

2   In Ex. 19:1 the Priestly Work explicitly places the stay on the mountain of God in the year of the exodus.

3   We can ignore the fanciful attempt made by Chapman 1935: 185ff.) to prove that the figure 480 is of Egyptian origin. But the common claim that 480 means simply a series of 12 generations, each lasting 40 years, is certainly wrong; for the figure 40 is too high for the interval between one generation and the next. The figure 40 is in fact used on occasion as a round number but with a quite different significance (see below pp.20f.). Furthermore, Dtr. based his chronology not on "generations" but on concrete figures and 480 must therefore fit in with these concrete figures.

4   In Bleek 1878: 184f.

5   Wellhausen 1895: 230f. [ET 1885: 229f.].

6   Wellhausen 1899: 213n.1.

7   1890: 135ff.; 1897: XVIIff.

8   On this assumption people think that the redactor responsible for the insertion of the "minor judges" naively believed that the sum total of the terms of office of the "minor judges" - amounting to 70 or, if we include Abimelech, 73 years (in fact 76 or 79, since one must also count the figure in Judg. 12:7) - should be included in the periods of foreign rule, a span of 71 years altogether. In fact, given the actual text and the arrangement of the whole work, one can include in the periods of foreign rule (Judg. 10:8; 13:1) at most the two series of "minor judges" in Judg. 10:1-5 and 12:8-15; but it proves impossible to include the first series, since the period of foreign rule is too short to accommodate it. So in both these passages one is obviously meant to count the periods of office of the "minor judges" as additional to the other periods given.

9   From Judg. 13:1 on, the situation is more complicated. See discussion below, pp.22f.

10   So, rightly, Chapman 1935: 185f. and J. de Koning 1940: 29f.

11   This figure was familiar to Dtr. in the tradition he knew; it is presupposed in Deut. 1:3; 2:14; Jos. 14:10.

12   The word dôr, usually translated by "generation", means the total group of contemporaries active in public life.

13   The time of rest is here made twice as long as usual, i.e., in view of what we have said above, it includes two complete changes of "generation". This is directly related to the statement in Judg. 3:31 on Shamgar, which gives no dates and which was therefore already part of Dtr.'s version. Dtr.

probably considered that Shamgar appeared halfway through the 80 year period.

14   Here, instead of giving a "time of rest" after Jephthah's victory, Dtr. gives us Jephthah's period of office as a "judge". This puts Jephthah on a par with the "minor judges"; see further below, p.43.

15   The assumption that an older introduction to the account of Philistine oppression was suppressed by the short statement in Judg. 13:1 (so Budde 1897: 92) is arbitrary. In fact Dtr. found no information on this point in the traditional account and so, in keeping with his practice elsewhere, inserted the round number 40 for the period of Philistine rule.

16   As is also suggested by de Koning (1940: 425).

17   The events reported in 1 Sam. 4-6 should be imagined as following each other closely within a single year.

18   The figure 40 itself, and the fact that 1 Sam. 4:18b is a secondary interpolation into a continuous narrative taken from an old source, show that there is no old tradition here. Elsewhere Dtr. has based his information concerning the periods of office of the "judges" on the tradition at his disposal.

19   He does not say when the 40 years began; this must mean that Dtr. tacitly assumes that a definite era began with the exodus from Egypt (as indicated by 1 Kings 6:1). The context of Deut. 1:3 strongly argues for the stay on Horeb as the starting point but, in any case, this is seen as following closely on the exodus.

20   Dtr. naturally dated the sending out of the spies from Kadesh in the year of the exodus; in particular the 40 years of wandering in the desert is reckoned as beginning from this expedition. Deut. 2:14 says that the interval between the departure from Kadesh and the crossing of the valley of Zered was 38 years. This means that the long stay in Kadesh in Deut. 1:46 is assumed to have lasted 2 years.

21   Jos. 14:6-14 is now part of the section Jos. 13-21, which was probably added to Dtr.'s work later. Originally, though, these verses perhaps were linked to Jos. 11 (see below, pp.40f.). In any case Dtr. considered that it belonged to the end of the occupation story.

22   Part of this formula was information on the kings' ages at accession. Dtr. had no information on this point for Saul, so he left the formula incomplete at this point.

23   Because of the fact mentioned above in n.22, it is improbable that Dtr. would have invented the length of Saul's

reign simply in order to arrrive at the 480 years given in 1 Kings 6:1.

24   The Philistines would not have let much time elapse between Saul's successful attack on the Philistine garrison at the beginning of his reign and their great counter-attack which led to the downfall of Saul. The idyllic folk-tale of 1 Sam. 9:1ff. should not mislead us into thinking that Saul's reign was long enough for him to develop from a youth into the father of grown-up sons. 1 Sam. 13:2ff. shows that Saul had sons of military age at the beginning of his reign.

25   The most substantial objection against attributing the figure to an original source is that in the chronology of the books of Samuel and Kings two years is regularly expressed with the dual of "year", but here it is expressed by "two" (so Driver 1913: 97). But the discrepancy can readily be accounted for by the diversity of Dtr.'s sources (cf. also 2 Sam. 2:10). Moreover, the normal use of language would require us to understand the plural of "year" in 1 Sam. 13:1b as a number between 2 and 10, not a number over 10.

26   This round figure could be the work of Dtr. who probably inserted it at 2 Sam. 5:4-5. For the length of David's stay in Hebron, Dtr. would have apparently had access to a particular source. This latter figure comes in very abruptly alongside some other chronological information in 2 Sam. 2:10a-11, a passage probably interpolated by Dtr. into the traditional narrative.

27   Cf. Begrich 1929: 90ff.

28   This figure appears in 1 Kings 6:37f., as part of an old text.

29   In any case this is how the supplementer of Jos. 13-21 (for this see below, pp.40f.) understood him, for he anticipated Jos. 23:1b in Jos. 13:1a and so transferred the division of the land and with it the end of the 45 year period from Jos. 14:10 to a point just before Joshua's death.

30   The statements of Dtr. in Judg. 2:9-10 could have implied a 40 year "time of rest" after the completion of the occupation; and, before Jos. 13-21 was incorporated, Dtr. contained a passage, closely preceding Judg. 2:9-10, which spoke of the peace that followed the distribution of all the land (Jos. 11:23b). When, contrary to his practice in corresponding statements in Judges (Judg. 3:11,30; 5:31; 8:28), Dtr. here gives no chronological information, there is probably a specific reason.

Notes to Chapter Five
THE HISTORY OF THE MOSAIC PERIOD

1   That is, what are commonly called the old "Hexateuchal"
sources. These are based on a combination of the "Sinai tradition" and the "occupation tradition" and the amalgamation of
these with ("pre-history" and) "patriarchal history" (cf. von Rad
1938 [ET 1966]).

2   On the relation of the content of the speech to that of
the subsequent narrative, see above pp.14f.

3   We cannot and need not examine more closely the
difficult problems of detail in the analysis of the "Hexateuch"
(especially difficult where Numbers is concerned).

4   Verse 5, apart from l'mr at the end, is an interpolation
which disturbs the syntax and, contrary to Dtr.'s intention,
mentions the law at this early stage and hence sees Deut. 1-3(4)
as a speech introducing the law; thus it already took the same
view of things as most scholars do now; the glossator derived
the rare verb b'r from Deut. 27:8. But v.4, which fits in with
Dtr. in its form and subject matter, is also probably an addition,
since l'mr (v.5) awkwardly disturbs the sense of v.3 and
inappropriately anticipates matters which are to be given in
greater detail later.

5   On the site of Beth-Peor, cf. Noth 1938a: 52. Dtr.
intended the "valley opposite Beth-Peor" to be a vague reference, as he thought that it was the same place as the grave of
Moses, the location of which was not known in his time (Deut.
34:6).

6   In Deut. 1:1 the expressions "in the wilderness" and
"beyond the Jordan" conflict with each other. "Beyond the
Jordan" expresses Dtr.'s meaning, since this is where the history
narrated in Jos. 1ff. begins. Therefore "in the wilderness" is
part of the traditional topographical information, while "beyond
the Jordan" was inserted by Dtr. Now the numerous unknown
names in Deut. 1:1 cannot be accommodated in the region of
Beth-Peor - we know a considerable amount about the original
settlement of Beth-Peor - or in the neighbouring region "beyond
the Jordan". As Musil (1907: 211) rightly recognised, these
names point to the region of the later desert castle of Meshetta
east of Madeba as does the notation "in the wilderness", which

makes sense in the light of what we have said. Suph should be identified with the present-day Khirbet Sufe, seven kilometres south-east of Madeba, and is probably mentioned here as a place on the eastern border of the settled arable region. Pharan is obviously brought in as the southern boundary of the wilderness area which Dtr. wants to delineate but it cannot now be located. As for the four places adduced to indicate the northern boundary, Musil is certainly right in locating the second and fourth (Laban = Khirbet Ellibben, a good twelve kilometres northwest of Meshetta; Di Zahab = ed-Dhebe, a good eight kilometres north-north-east of Meshetta), whereas we cannot be sure of the other two places. The reference in v.2, "eleven days journey from Horeb by the way of Mount Seir", may also come from the topographical description taken over by Dtr., since it is inconceivable that Dtr. could have arrived at this information by himself. On the other hand, the notation at the end of the verse, "to Kadesh-barnea", was certainly the work of a later commentator who wanted to make it quite clear that the Israelite tribes did not go from Horeb to the place in question directly but went to the oasis of Kadesh first.

7   There is no reason to attribute the chronological data in v.32 to the "priestly writer" rather than to Dtr., since Dtr. is no less interested in chronology than is the "priestly writer". The variation from v.2 in the expression used for "eleven" can be explained satisfactorily, if v.2 came into Dtr.'s history from an unknown older source.

8   This is also mentioned in Ex. 32:34; 33:1, but in completely different language.

9   In the whole of Dtr. the name Sinai appears only in Judg. 5:5 in the song of Deborah, which comes from the old tradition, and there it is clearly a later gloss. But cf., for the opposite view, Albright 1935: 204.

10   In Ex. 3:1 the mention of the name "Horeb" following the "mountain of God" can be proved on stylistic evidence to be an addition. "At Horeb" in Ex. 17:6 is very obviously an addition; scholars make unconvincing attempts to clear up the stylistic difficulty of the passage by analysing it according to its sources. Finally in Ex. 33:6 the almost unintelligible "from the mountain of Horeb" is again a clumsy interpolation. Furthermore, analysis of Ex. 33 according to its sources rests upon very shaky ground.

11   One might think that Dtr. took the name Horeb from the Elijah story re-worked by him later in 1 Kings 19:8, except that

the word "Horeb" here looks like a note added by Dtr. to the term "mountain of God", and the Deuteronomic law contains the name. In the passage discussed above (Deut. 1:1-2a), where the name Horeb appears, we apparently have a fragment of the lost source from which the Deuteronomic law and Dtr. and also Mal. 3:22 and Ps. 106:19 derived this name.

12   Gen. 10:16; 15:21; Ex. 3:8,17; 13:5; 23:23; 33:2; 34:11; Num. 13:29.

13   Num. 21:13,21,25,26,29,31,32,34; 22:2; 32:33,39. But cf. Noth 1940c: 182ff. "Amorite" in Gen. 14:7,13 comes from a different source.

14   On the "compiler" of the occupation tradition, see Noth 1938a: XIf.

15   In Deut. 1:7 the connection between the various geographical details is not quite clear. Dtr. refers to the whole promised land as "the hill-country of the Amorites" (vv. 19,20) and evidently felt it necessary to elaborate this term by enumerating the "neighbours"; this end is served by the topographical descriptions even though "the hill country" is mentioned again in these descriptions. Dtr.'s general use of the name "Amorite" (Deut. 1:27, etc.) is based on this application of the term "hill country of the Amorites" but, apart from this, there is a precedent in the history of the occupation (except for the passages mentioned above, cf. Jos. 7:7).

16   The phrase "the land of the Canaanites" is obviously a gloss.

17   In Jos. 1:4 Dtr. uses this expression again, and Jos. 1:4-5a was subsequently inserted on the analogy of Deut. 11:24-25a as is shown by the similarity of the wording and by the fact that Deut. 11:24-25a fits awkwardly into its context and looks like an interpolation. The Euphrates is mentioned as a boundary in Gen. 15:18, another interpolation, and in Ex. 23:31 in a secondary passage influenced by Dtr. Moreover, 1 Kings 5:1, cited above, may not be pre-Deuteronomistic.

18   The relative clause v.8b[b], in itself typically Deuteronomistic in wording and subject matter, must be recognised as an addition, because Yahweh appears in the third person.

19   For details, cf. especially Steuernagel 1923: 51f.

20   The original text does not include v.21 because of the unmotivated use of the singular form of address, "the cities are great and fortified up to heaven" in v.28 (probably taken over from 9:1), v.31a (singular address), v.33 (an inappropriate

repetition of v.30a based on Ex. 13:21; Num. 10:33), "this evil generation" in v.35, vv.37,38 (anticipating 3:26,28), v.39aa (from Num. 14:31).

21   In Num. 13:14 we cannot disentangle the pre-exilic sources since the whole passage is influenced by the account in the priestly work on which it is based.

22   This emerges from the use of several singular expressions here, e.g. rgn (not found anywhere else in the historical books), mss hi. (apart from here, not found in the historical books except in another passage by Dtr., Jos. 14:8), hwn (found nowhere else), the picture of the bees in v.44 (here only).

23   The statement here that the "hill-country of the Amorites" extends to Kadesh (1:20) clearly indicates that Dtr. meant the "hill-country of the Amorites" to cover the whole of Palestine, at the extreme south of which in fact lies the oasis of Kadesh.

24   Since the "good" report of the spies (v.25) meets with immediate popular opposition (vv.26-27) Dtr. would have meant by v.28 that the people made their own interpretation of the detailed narrative of the spies which was meant to be "good" and interesting and thereby demoralised all the spies except Caleb.

25   Verse 36 cannot be secondary since Caleb's exceptional conduct is the crux of the whole story and Dtr. needed to mention him because of Jos. 14:6-14. The appearance of Yahweh in the third person at the end of the verse is probably due to a simple textual error (cf. BH³, ad loc.); otherwise the explanatory sentence, but this sentence only, would have to be by a later hand.

26   The arrangement of Horeb, Kadesh and the "hill country of the Amorites" in a simple line suggests that Dtr., who certainly knew where Kadesh was, attempted to place Horeb in what is today called the Sinai peninsula.

27   In v.8a we must read 't not m't since the preceding passage says that they went through the Edomite region; the text was later altered to take the tribes past the Edomite region (with Num. 20:21b in mind).

28   The usual textual alteration of midderek in v.8a is unfounded and wrong. In Dtr.'s view the Israelites emphatically do not go north, taking the road through Arabah, as one would expect them to do in their journey from el-Aqaba to Palestine (cf. Num. 33:35b,36a,41bff., and thereon Noth 1940a: 16ff.).

Instead, according to v.1b, they start from the Reed Sea and go around to Edom on the east side. Besides, if the Israelites had taken the Arabah road, they could not have begun by going towards the wilderness of Moab, as Dtr. makes them do in Deut. 2:8a,b on their way through Edomite territory.

29   For the meaning of the word drk in Deut. 2:8b, cf. Deut. 1:19. Here it does not mean "the road through the wilderness of Moab" but "the road towards the wilderness of Moab".

30   "The valley of Zered" appears in only one other passage, Num. 21:12b, which seems to be derived from this passage, as it comes in a very fragmentary section depending on secondary borrowings. Num. 21:10-12a comes from Num. 33:43b-45a; hence Num. 21 can not help us to explain the name. Some think that "valley of Zered" here means the system of the Sel el-Mujjib or one of its parts, and therefore the southern boundary of the area later settled by the Israelite tribes, and that v.24a^a must therefore also be secondary (so Steuernagel, ad loc.); but this overlooks the fact that "Arnon" is used in the Old Testament and by Dtr. himself (cf. Deut. 3:8 etc.) in a general sense to mean the system of Sel el-Mujjib and therefore there would be no point in having a different name. Dtr. must have considered the Zered valley to be a valley system further south.

31   The route of the wandering is clearly specified, in contrast to the vague and contradictory information accumulated in the various layers of composition in the books of Exodus to Numbers. This seems to be the contribution of Dtr. himself who constructed a definite picture out of the information in the traditions.

32   The use of the singular form of address proves that this half-verse is an addition.

33   The conclusion from Num. 20:14-21, that Israel finally retreated, without putting up a fight, in the face of Edomite resistance, was untenable for Dtr. because in 2:2ff. he says that the journey through Edom was expressly commanded by God, and Edomite hostility could not have frustrated the execution of the command.

34   It is hard to say to what extent Dtr. had in mind Deut. 23:4-8a in his account of these events, because we do not know how many of the additions to the text of the law in Deut. 23:5-7 existed before Dtr. The latest addition (vv.5b-6) was probably not known to Dtr. But if he had read v.5a(7), he might have interpreted the text as showing that the Israelite tribes did not go through the land of the Moabites and the Ammonites, but

only passed close by.

35   The references to the oldest inhabitants of the regions east of the Jordan obviously follow autochthonous popular traditions; but, since they put Yahweh in the third person (vv.10-12,20-23), they are generally and rightly regarded as later additions here. The same is true of v.7, expressed in the singular, and the passage vv.24a^{b}b-25 which inappropriately anticipates what is about to be narrated.

36   ^{c}th in v.13 probably came in along with the addition v.9a^{b}b.

37   These include Ps. 135:11; 136:20; as well as Neh. 9:22; and Num. 21:33; 32:33; which are evidently later additions based on Dtr.

38   The interpolations in this passage include vv.30b,31 (for v.30b, cf. above p.30) and v.37, as shown by the singular form of address; and also v.29b^b, as Steuernagel (ad loc.) rightly deduces from the use of the first person plural instead of the first person singular; moreover v.29b^b gives the false impression that the promised land was originally confined to the region west of the Jordan and extended later only de facto as a result of the behaviour of the Transjordanian kings.

39   In this passage v.2 is an addition; it has the singular form of address and anticipates v.3.

40   Verse 29 must not be classed with v.9 as secondary, since v.8b tells us that the Israelites still went on through the "wilderness of Moab". In the light of what we have said, v.29 is an important statement in the context of Dtr.'s general outlook. Dtr., and after him the supplementer in 2:9,18, probably took ^{c}r, as a geographical name for the Moabite territory, from the old poetic passages Num. 21:15 and 28, just as in 2:36 and 3:4 he borrowed the rare word qryh from Num. 21:28.

41   In the case of Jericho, a special stipulation is made in view of the later Achan story (Jos. 6:17,19).

42   For this formula, cf. 2 Sam. 24:5 (emended text). The formulation in Deut. 2:36 does not then need to be traced back to Jos. 13:16 and the passages derived from it; and therefore it need not be classed, like Jos. 13ff., as a secondary element within Dtr., since 2 Sam. 24:5 shows that this form of expression had become standard long since.

43   For the variation in the meaning of the name "Gilead", cf. Noth 1941: 51ff.

44   The relative clause with the phrase "beyond the Jordan", not appropriate to Moses , may well be a later addition.

113

The Deuteronomistic History

45   The territories of the tribes of Reuben and Gad are not yet distinguished from one another; cf. on this, Noth 1935: 239.

46   The phrase "the kingdom of Og" in v.13a, which does not have a counterpart in the parallel v.12, could of course be an explanatory addition.

47   Og here is included in the "aboriginal population", in contradistinction to Sihon; this can only be explained by the fact that his land, Bashan, contained a Canaanite urban civilisation which survived into the Late Bronze Age. The autochthonous Transjordanian popular traditions about an "aboriginal population" apparently linked themselves onto the very diverse and ancient remnants of the Copper and Bronze Age civilisation in that country.

48   So, rightly, Steuernagel, ad loc.

49   According to the later tradition in Num. 32:17ff. it was the Transjordanian tribes' own idea to volunteer further help.

50   Cf. above p.28 on Deut. 1:26ff.

51   It is significant that here Dtr. does not yet assume the doctrine of strictly individual retribution.

52   That applies to vv.9,19,20 (which is a later addition to v.19 despite its plural form of address), 23b^b,24 and, above all, the final section, vv.29-40 (the first verb in v.29 was also originally in the second singular), which in v.38 assumes that the occupation has already taken place and betrays its context, showing the influence of later writing; e.g. in v.32 the allusion to Gen. 1 and in v.32 and v.34 the use of the word 'lhym instead of the name yhwh.

53   Steuernagel, ad loc., rightly regards vv.3-4 as secondary, referring to a story, found in Num. 25, which Dtr. does not tell. Verse 21 was added later to explain v.22 and is not formally connected with it.

54   In v.10 we should read with the Septuagint ᶜmdtm and 'lhykm.

55   This version appears in Deut. 5:19 and hence was known to Dtr.

56   The word "covenant" here no longer means "covenant act" or "covenant relationship" but has the secondary sense of "divine law" (cf. Noth 1940b: 78 [ET 1966: 38]).

57   Both v.21 and vv.19-20 are certainly later (cf. notes 52 and 53 above) and, given their subject matter, cannot be intended to link up with the explanatory sentence v.22.

58   Similarly v.23b and v.25b^a must also go. In v.25b the double wᶜaśytm is stylistically unacceptable.

59   The beginning of v.25 originally had the plural twlydw.

60   In v.5 the perfect lmdty should be understood as perfectum declarativum.

61   Verses 3a,4,6b are shown by the use of the singular to be the secondary form of address and their position before v.8 is awkward. In this passage not only v.3b, anticipating v.7, but also vv.5-6a are later additions.

62   It is not clear that v.9a^a and Deut. 9:9-10:5 contradict each other (so Steuernagel, ad loc.) since, in the former the decalogue is meant, but in the latter the Deuteronomic law. Verse 9a^bb could be an addition since the expression "the priests, the sons of Levi, who carried the ark of the covenant of Yahweh" does not occur elsewhere in Dtr.

63   Verses 11a^a and 12a are later because of the singular form of address in them.

64   Instead of the "Levites, who bear the ark of the covenant of Yahweh" (v.25) Dtr. speaks elsewhere, when using the same formula, of "priests" (Jos. 3:8 and passim). If vv.24-26a was also added later, then even so vv.*9-13 must have been inserted still later because of the connection between v.24 and v.9a^a.

65   Deut. 31:26b,27a have the singular form of address and are even later. Staerk (1894: 75), followed by recent commentators, arbitrarily assumes that v.24 originally contained hšyrh instead of htwrh, an assumption that has done nothing but confuse the literary analysis of Deut. 31-32.

66   This passage certainly comes from an earlier source but in this context is secondary in a literary sense.

Notes to Chapter Six
THE OCCUPATION OF THE LAND WEST OF THE JORDAN

1   Möhlenbrink (1938: 240) has quite correctly pointed out that, when the separate aetiological legends came into being, it was already assumed that the immigrants had waged a campaign of conquest. The "question" of the course and results of this campaign was first raised by the compiler of these legends.

2   On the work of the "compiler" of these traditions and his date (c.900 B.C.), cf. Noth 1938a: XIf.

3   We do not propose to discuss at this point the details of the older sources re-worked by Dtr. We note briefly that Dtr. was elsewhere demonstrably in a position to use older inde-

pendent complexes of tradition for his history; this would suggest that he had access to the occupation tradition in such a form. In any case, detailed analysis does not support but rather undermines (cf. Noth 1938a: XIII) the thesis that the occupation tradition adapted by Dtr. had anything to do with one of the "Hexateuchal" sources. Möhlenbrink (p.267), too, thinks that the complete complex of occupation traditions came into being prior to the "Hexateuchal" sources; the connection he later makes between the two is therefore unfounded.

4 Verses 7-9 are later; but vv.5b^{b}b-6 could belong to the original text of Dtr. (against Noth 1938a: ad loc.).

5 For literary criticism of this section, cf. Noth 1938a: ad loc.

6 The other additions in 2:9-11 (cf. Noth 1938a: ad loc.) are probably later.

7 Verse 4a was added even later. In v.2 Dtr. brings in the "officers" of Deut. 1:15, similarly in Jos. 1:10.

8 The transformation of the original "ark of Yahweh" into an "ark of the covenant of Yahweh" in Jos. 3:4, which is achieved rather carelessly and inconsistently, may well be the work not of Dtr., but of a later writer who based it on Dtr.'s additions to the text.

9 For the ^{c}d-tm in v.6, cf. the occurrence of this word twice over in Deut. 2:14-15; as well as in 2:16, as indeed also in Num. 14:33 and, on the other side, Jos. 8:24; 10:20.

10 Möhlenbrink (1938: 244, 266) has treated Jos. 8:30-35 as part of the old tradition (similarly sections of Jos. 1) without giving any explanation; but it is quite impossible to justify this. Since we are here concerned not with the history and pre-history of the old traditions but with Dtr.'s work, this is not the place for detailed treatment of Möhlenbrink's article on the occupation legends of the Book of Joshua. We shall deal with this later and give his results the attention they deserve.

11 This is valid even if one takes into account that Jos. 8:30-35 (cf. Noth 1938a: ad loc.) as well as Deut. 27:2ff. were augmented secondarily and, in particular, that the later additions in Jos. 8:30-35 have been determined by Deut. 27:2-8 but also by Deut. 27:11-13. For the parts of Jos. 8:30ff. which definitely belong to the original text show how dependent it is on Deut. 27:2ff. and it is worth asking whether Jos. 8:33a^a could be a variation of Deut. 27:11-13 and an adaptation of the passage which stands on its own in Deut. 27, to fit what is previously said in Jos. 8:30ff.

12   It makes little real difference whether Jos. 8:30-35 originally came before or after 9:1,2 (so the Septuagint). The old occupation tradition did not know of a conquest of the hill-country of Ephraim; the conquest was assumed to follow naturally from the defeat of the city of Ai.

13   Cf. Noth 1938a: 57f.

14   The phrase 'yš h'lhym in v.6, used instead of ᶜbd yhwh, Dtr.'s normal wording elsewhere, is probably taken from a source.

15   On the literary growth of Jos. 12:1-6, cf. Noth 1938a: 45.

16   The stereotyped list of nations in v.8b is probably secondary.

17   This list is not complete and is therefore not made up very carefully. After v.12a Libnah (of 10:29-30) is missing and so is Hazor (of 11:10ff.) after v.13. Verse 12b suggests that Dtr. had 10:33 before him in the old history of the occupation with its secondary mention of Gezer, but he seems unaware of 10:28 with its secondary reference to the conquest of Makkedah.

18   Jos. 21:1-42 and 22:7-34 are even later interpolations.

19   On the earlier history of this description of the possessions of the tribes, cf. Noth 1938a: IXf. (with further bibliography).

20   Jos. 13-14:1ff. was later mutilated by various interpolations and by a later writer, who transferred various elements to follow Num. 32,34. See further, pp.194f., 198 n.4 [of Überlieferungsgeschichtliche Studien].

21   Apart from vv.1b,2abᵃ,4b which are definitely additions, the remarks about the number of tribes (vv.3b,4a) may well have been added later.

22   On the other hand, Jos. 15:13-19 was not inserted until later to agree with Judg. 1; similarly Jos. 13-22 was glossed to agree with Judg. 1.

23   For details, cf. Noth 1938a: 95ff.

24   The transferral of the scene to Shiloh (18:1) is secondary.

Notes to Chapter Seven
THE PERIOD OF THE JUDGES

1   Literary analysis does not indicate such a number of pre-Deuteronomistic "sources" which are used consistently throughout. In the original text, the Ehud story is homogeneous,

the Deborah-Barak story consists of a single prose narrative and the song of Deborah (thus not two "sources"), the Gideon story is compiled from at least two longer narrative threads and various separate fragments, in the Jephthah story there is a homogeneous groundwork, expanded later with supplementary material including Judg. 11:12-28 which was presumably introduced later than Dtr., and separate stories, and finally, the Samson story is made up of a series of loosely connected separate stories, each of which is self-contained.

2   In any case we cannot prove the connecting passages in the text as we have it show any sign of pre-Deuteronomistic composition. Of course, the stories of heroes would not have existed in total isolation before Dtr.'s time; they are linked with one another in that they treat the same theme. Presumably Dtr. like other writers took the specific information about the duration of each period of foreign rule (Judg. 3:8,14; 4:3; 6:1; 10:8), which is found in the connecting passages of his own composition, from the old tradition; presumably then the old heroic stories had some kind of brief introduction which has been replaced by Dtr.'s connecting text.

3   Cf. Alt 1934: 31ff. [ET 1966: 102].

4   We need not here present a detailed argument against the deletion of the "minor judges" from the Deuteronomistic Book of Judges. The argument has been supplied implicitly in the points made above in the text.

5   The short term of office is perfectly consistent with the terms of office given in Judg. 12:8-15.

6   It so happens that the text with the name of the burial-place in Judg. 12:7 has been mutilated and cannot be definitively reconstructed; the information given in several Septuagint manuscripts (cf. BH^3, ad loc.) may be only a guess.

7   It is theoretically possible that both complexes of tradition could have mentioned two different persons with the same name and that Dtr.'s history of the "judges" may, in consequence, have at its core a mistaken conflation of two figures with the same name. However, this is unlikely since Judg. 12:7 explicitly calls Jephthah a Gileadite and so agrees with the great heroic narrative.

8   We may ask whether Dtr. knew the heroic stories in a fixed sequence with Jephthah in the final position. In any case Dtr. could have independently put the heroic stories first and only then given the "(minor) judges", among which he had to find a place for Jephthah. Kuenen (1890: 11f. n.7) has rightly

118

pointed out that Jephthah belongs to the group of the "minor judges".

9   This is the case only with Deborah (Judg. 4:5).

10   Grether 1939: 110ff.

11   The addition in 2:17 also uses this technical term.

12   The passages are collected in Eissfeldt 1925: 12f.

13   So Wiese 1926: 5 n.1. Wiese, as opposed to Eissfeldt (loc. cit.) is certainly right to argue that, in assessing the occurrence of "Israel" in the heroic stories from the point of view of literary criticism, we cannot account for it as an accretion from the "Hexateuchal" sources added to the original text in Judges.

14   The conventional formula used to report the times of "rest" is very similar to the text of Jos. 11:23b (=14:15b); this shows that both passages are by the same author (Dtr.).

15   It is unthinkable that Jephthah as well as Othniel were found by Dtr. both in the list of "judges" and as the subjects of an heroic narrative; nothing is said of the term of office as "judge" and besides there seems to be no reason why Dtr. should have omitted a traditional heroic story, telling us nothing but a few names. The tradition concerning this Othniel (Jos. 15:15-19 = Judg. 1:11-15) was not known to Dtr. (Judg. 3:9b[b] was probably added later) and gives Othniel a totally different role. In fact Othniel's opponent in Judg. 3:7-11 is even more obscure than Othniel himself.

16   Cf. above chapter 4, n.13 and below p.51 (on 1 Sam. 12:9).

17   Verse 1b is a later addition and v.3b obviously comes from the old tradition; here the information on the duration of the period of foreign rule has probably retained its original context, whereas elsewhere Dtr. puts such information in his own words (3:8b,14; 6:1).

18   On Dtr.'s use of h'mry in v.10, cf. above pp.27f.

19   Dtr. introduces his references to the first two "(minor) judges" in Judg. 10:1,3 with wyqm. This is related to the "raising up of the heroes" treated hitherto (cf. 3:9,15; also 2:16,18). In Judg. 12:8,11,13, on the other hand, he follows the text of the old "judges" tradition.

20   In the old tradition the two stories were probably linked only by the name Jerubbaal, which is the name of Abimelech's father in Judg. 9 and the name later given to Gideon, in Judg. 6:25-32. The old tradition already regarded the two as one and the same person.

21   Dtr. does not mention him by name in v.27b, probably

deliberately.

22   Verse 29 originally served as a conclusion to the separate story, 6:25-32. Later it was used as the final sentence in the old compilation of the Gideon story and, by mentioning the name Jerubbaal at this point, it linked the story directly with 9:1ff. According to the old Gideon tradition, his name, from 6:32 on, was in fact Jerubbaal. Following the narrative of the great heroes, the name Gideon is still used thereafter; but at the beginning of the description of the battle in 7:1 Jerubbaal is used again explicitly as the real name of Gideon. Dtr., on the other hand, uses the name Gideon when he is writing independently (8:27b-28,30-35); in 8:30-31 the subject matter of his preliminaries to the Abimelech story is completely derived from Judg. 9.

23   The Philistines are mentioned before the Ammonites in v.7 because of an error, possibly simply the result of the juxtaposition of the two names at the end of v.6.

24   The land of the "Amorites" in v.8 should be taken in this special sense.

25   In v.8 wyrṣṣw 't-bny yśr'l bšnh hhy' was added later, probably through development from the variant wyrṣṣw for wyrᶜṣw.

26   In vv.11-12 the text as we have it is corrupt, obviously because the verb after wmn-h'mry accidentally dropped out and mn was erroneously put in before the two names which followed. In vv.11bᵇ-12aᵃ, where the text is probably even more corrupt than it looks, Dtr. is at all events looking back briefly over the content of the book of Judges thus far; "Amalek and 'Midian' " refers to Gideon, the "Sidonians" to Jabin and Sisera, the "Philistines" to Shamgar, and originally "Moab" referred to Ehud; but as in Judg. 11:12-28 this "Moab" was secondarily changed to "Ammonites" by a later author influenced by the importance of the Ammonites for Jephthah.

27   In this context, Judg. 11:12-28 is a separate section and was probably interpolated after Dtr's day. The strange confusion of "Ammonites" with "Moab" in this passage is best explained if we date it in the time when "Ammon" was the name of the province bordering the province of Judah on the east and including the region between the Arnon, the Jabbok and the Jordan, which according to Judg. 11:12-28 was originally the subject of contention and previously temporarily occupied by Moab (cf. Alt 1931: 70f.). It does not help matters to change "Ammonite" to "Moab" in Judg. 11:12-28, as is usually

done, for this does not explain how this section came into the Jephthah story which is otherwise only about the Ammonites (for Aroer in Judg. 11:33, cf. "Aroer which lies over against Rabbah" in Jos. 13:25). The two names in this section are therefore confused with one another from the beginning and the confusion is best accounted for by the historical situation mentioned above. Moreover this chapter uses material from the various Pentateuchal traditions (but cf. Deut. 2:2ff.). The main Jephthah story contained no mention of its hero's homeland; in Judg. 11:1b 'yš probably stood before gl^{c}d (and so vv.1b-2a: "a Gileadite was the father of Jephthah, and a Gileadite woman bore him further sons also"; for this use of 'yš followed by a proper name, cf. Judg. 10:1; 1 Sam. 4:12).

28   For its earlier history, cf. in particular Rost 1926.

29   For Judg. 13-16 and 1 Sam. 1-3, see below pp.52f. It is recognised that Judg. 17-21 was not part of Dtr.'s work but was added later.

30   Wellhausen 1899: 239ff., especially 243.

31   Cf. Eissfeldt 1934: 306f. [ET: 272f.]; Weiser 1939: 127 [ET: 161f.].

32   The old expressions "ark of Yahweh" and "ark of God" are rather inconsistently replaced by the Deuteronomistic "ark of the covenant of Yahweh"; here, as in Jos. 3-4 this is probably the work of a later author, as is the insertion of 4:18b (cf. above p.22), the more so because Dtr.'s normal practice would be to put this chronological reference at the end of ch. 4. "Levites" in 6:15 was also probably added later.

33   We must stress that this formula, used four times in ch. 7 (vv.6,15,16,17) makes sense only in the light of Dtr.'s own picture of the "judges" period; this emerges from the object "Israel" and from the fact that, particularly in v.6, it is not a question of judicial activity but of leading the people.

34   The specific reference to the place Mizpah is probably based on a local tradition which may originally have dealt with the material upon which the report in 1 Sam. 10:17ff. is based (for this, cf. p.50 and n.36 below).

35   For thunder as a divine manifestation, cf. in Dtr. 1 Sam. 12:18; for the use of hmm in the traditional materials used by Dtr. see Jos. 10:10, Judg. 4:15, and in Dtr. himself see Deut. 2:15. The language of 1 Sam. 7:10 is reminiscent of Ps. 18:14-15; perhaps Dtr. was familiar with this psalm.

36   The topographical information in 1 Sam. 7:11b-12a, which we cannot explain further, is doubtless based on a local

tradition of Mizpah, according to which this stone was probably already associated with Samuel. Dtr. was probably the first to interpret it as indicating victory over the Philistines and certainly the first to use the name 'bn h^{c}zr, the more so because 1 Sam. 4:1 and 5:1 give a completely different location.

37   In so doing Dtr. took insufficient account of the tradition which he later used in 1 Sam. 13:2ff., perhaps considering what was said there a mere detail which could not seriously affect the statement of v.13b which referred only to Samuel's lifetime, whereas he thought that the statement in v.13a referred only to the short-term consequences of the great victory over the Philistines. In v.14 the Philistine cities of Ekron and Gath are declared to be Israelite possessions, a statement which could agree with Jos. 11:22, if the name Gath were deleted from the latter, following LXX^B (only the city of Ashkelon would then be disregarded in both passages). In v.14 Dtr. uses the name "Amorite" in the sense he normally gives it (cf. above pp.27f.).

38   For the expression "he judged Israel" in vv.15-17, cf. above n.33. The city Ramah (= er-Ram) as the home of Samuel (v.17) is derived from 1 Sam. 1:19; 2:11. The names of the other places in v.16 are, however, obviously based on a Samuel tradition familiar to Dtr.

39   Cf. above pp.24f.

40   Again, Dtr. probably took the names of Samuel's sons and the fact of their activity in Beersheba from an old tradition.

41   Dtr. uses the old traditional material to portray the heroes of the "judges" period as charismatic leaders. He tends to see them, by association with the "(minor) judges", as holders of a specific office but he highlights the element of divine vocation. He sees the monarchy as nothing more than a self-appointed, permanent institution and, understandably enough, he has the Judaean monarchy in mind and disregards the charismatic element in the Israelite monarchy.

42   The only specific traditional detail is the shifting of the scene to Ramah. But another tradition made Ramah the domicile of Samuel (see above, n.38).

43   Eissfeldt 1931: 7f.

44   Saul's height, obviously a historical fact, is also mentioned in 9:2, there too in the same traditional words, but without the suggestion that it contributed to his accession.

45   In the Samuel-Saul story Mizpah occurs only in the sections for which Dtr. himself is responsible. Dtr. must have

used a tradition which differed from the Samuel-Saul story we know to have made this place the seat of assembly of the people; Mizpah has this function as early as 1 Sam. 7.

46   This can be disputed because of the difference in expression and because it was scarcely necessary to proclaim the law of the king in 10:25a after 8:11ff., even if the audience in ch.10 is different from that in ch.8.

47   The surprising reference to the clan of Matar in v.21a (the conclusion of which should be supplemented following LXX) cannot be disposed of by emendation of the text (contrary to the view of BH³, ad loc.); in the old account adapted by Dtr. the clan of Matar must have been mentioned in Saul's family tree.

48   Eissfeldt (1931) is absolutely right to argue against the usual view of 10:25b-27a as an editorial parenthesis, as is apparent from what is actually said in the passage.

49   Dtr. had to obscure the original sense of 11:14,15 to fit in with 10:17ff.; he did so by means of the unmotivated and awkward statement that the point now was nothing more than a "renewal of the kingdom".

50   The phrase "and Yahweh sent Moses and Aaron" (v.8) is a later addition from Jos. 24:5. The next two verbs should be read in the third person singular - so LXX (only LXX^B differs in the first verb). In v.6, the relative clause about Moses and Aaron, with its very strange wording is also an addition.

51   The unintelligible "Bedan" in v.11 goes back to an original "Gideon" (the "Barak" of LXX is only guesswork); then "Jerubbaal" can be read as an obvious addition to "Gideon".

52   Changing "Samuel", surprising in a speech by Samuel, to "Samson" (as LXX^bc [Brooke-McLean], Arm, Pesh) was such an obvious thing to do, that the lack of textual authority for this reading, as well as the principle of the lectio difficilior, argues for the authenticity of the Hebrew text. Samuel's reference to himself in the third person may be intended by Dtr. or else is the result of an oversight.

53   Cf. the expression used in the list of foreign rulers in Judg. 10:11-12, equally artificial in its own way.

54   Eissfeldt (1934: 294 [ET 1965: 262]) is wrong to see v.11 as isolated and unrelated to vv.9,10; he draws far-reaching literary-critical conclusions from this.

55   The reference to the new king as "Yahweh's anointed" could also be an allusion to 10:1.

56   In 1 Sam. 7:11b,12a,16. This Samuel tradition, too, seems

to be attached to Mizpah. But these traditional elements which Dtr. has adapted cannot be extracted from Dtr.'s text and connected to make an independent narrative.

57   Elsewhere too (cf. 1 and 2 Kings) Dtr. had access to various prophetic traditions. The story of the young Samuel may be one of these. The fact that this story represents Samuel as a prophet need not make Dtr.'s conception of Samuel as a "judge" misleading, since Deborah also was both prophet and "judge" (Judg. 4:4-5).

58   The reference to Samuel as a priest is based on the traditional accounts which, particularly in their later expanded form, saw Samuel as the counterpart to and successor of the sons of Eli (cf. 2:27-31,36). Dtr. has Samuel acting as a priest elsewhere too (cf. 7:9,17b); for Dtr. this did not conflict with his function as a "judge", either.

59   In 16:31b the statement takes the form of a noun clause with pluperfect sense. The repetition of these lines is not a discrepancy and does not have implications for literary criticism. These lines mean that Samson took office as "judge" for 20 years after his first actions (15:20), and that this office was confirmed retrospectively after his death (16:31b).

60   Dtr. would have altered the arrangement by transferring the term of office as "judge", here assigned to one of the heroes and precisely dated (on the analogy of Jephthah), to occur during a period of foreign rule.

Notes to Chapter Eight
SAUL, DAVID, SOLOMON

1   Apart from 1 Sam. 9:1-10:16 and 10:27b-11:15 this initially contained the story of the Philistine conflict in 1 Sam. 13-14. The story of the dispute between Saul and Samuel (1 Sam. 15) was added later and 1 Sam. 16:1-13, which tells of the final repudiation of Saul, was the final addition.

2   1 Sam. 16:14 - 2 Sam. 5:25 including various later additions especially in the first part of this account.

3   (1 Sam. 4:1b-7:1) and 2 Sam. 6-7,9-20 and 1 Kings 1-2 with the earlier literary sources used in these passages (more on this in Rost 1926). 2 Sam. 21-24 is full of additions, which gradually accumulated after Dtr.'s history had been divided into separate books. 2 Sam. 21:1-14 and 24:1-25 were the first

passages to be added, as we can tell from the thematic connection between 24:1a and 21:1-14. This connection was later broken by the interposition of the anecdotes and lists of David's "mighty men" (2 Sam. 21:15-22 and 23:8-39). This latter complex of traditional material, held together by its subject matter, was then split in two when the poetic passages (ch. 22 and 23:1-7) were inserted.

4   This is done in 1 Sam. 15; but it is particularly conspicuous in the first part of the story of David's rise.

5   Cf. 1 Kings 11:4; 15:3ff. inter alia.

6   See above pp.23f.

7   Dtr. skilfully incorporated this formulaic introduction into the old text at the point where the territories ruled by Eshbaal and David are described one after the other. But v.10a separates statements which originally belonged together and this shows that vv.10a and 11 are secondary literarily; they are to be attributed to Dtr.

8   The pattern of this formula is almost exactly the same as that used in 1 Sam. 13:1 and in the formulaic introductions to accounts of later Israelite or Judaean kings. It is not clear why Dtr. introduced the round number 40, probably not in the tradition, at 2 Sam. 2:10a whereas he omitted the figure for Saul's age at accession in 1 Sam. 13:1, presumably because of a gap in his source.

9   We cannot ascertain whether it was inserted before or after Dtr.

10   R. Kittel (in Kautzsch 1922-23: ad loc.) is probably the only person to suppose that it is by Dtr.

11   The list of David's sons in 2 Sam. 3:2-5 (with v.6a serving as a transition) is probably not part of the original tradition, but must have been inserted, together with the appendix 5:13-16, later (but surely prior to Dtr.), as referring to the story of the succession and drawing on an existing list.

12   In 1 Chron. 11:1-9, where 2 Sam. 5:1-10 is quoted according to Dtr.'s arrangement of the material, the formulaic introduction to the account of David is omitted. However, this does not prove that it was not in 2 Sam. 5 at the time of the Chronicler; more probably, he passed over it with 1 Chron. 29:26ff. in mind. In keeping with his normal practice Dtr. had to insert it at 2 Sam. 5.

13   Verse 17 and vv.1-3 are explicitly connected. This shows us that vv.17-25 originally came immediately after vv.1-3 and that vv.6-10 and 12 were not added until later; the latter

section ends with the concluding remarks on the history of David's rise which reaches its culmination at this point (on vv.13-16 see above, n.11).

14   The original ending was v.10. Verse 12 in which the further use of the name "Israel" is inconsistent with vv.1-3 was added later but still prior to Dtr. On the other hand, v.11 is about the building of David's palace in Jerusalem and was therefore inserted later on, when the rest of the story of David had been attached so that v.10(12) had ceased to function as a conclusion; the verse probably came in, at the earliest, with 8:1-14 and Dtr. could therefore have placed it in its present position (see below on ch.8, p.56).

15   1 Chron. 14:8 shows no knowledge of v.17b[b] and was not added until later and then with vv.6-10, which now precede it, in mind.

16   So Kuenen 1890: 47 n.5; Nowack 1902: ad loc.

17   Dtr. follows the tradition very closely in laying stress upon the person of King David but he is equally well quite incapable (see 1 Sam. 8-12) of approving of the monarchy as a permanent institution.

18   Rost 1926: 47ff.

19   For the expression (the "name" of Yahweh), which is Dtr.'s own, cf. in Dtr. in particular 1 Kings 5:17-19; 8:15-20 where, independently of any existing account, Dtr. was free to develop his reinterpretation of Nathan's prophecy, to which he refers.

20   To introduce v.13a Dtr. probably added v.12b rather than 13b (as Rost) since c_d-c_{wlm} in the latter cannot be Dtr.'s own wording.

21   Rost 1926: 49. For the Deuteronomistic style of these verses, cf. Deut. 4:7-8; 10:21; 28:9; 29:12; 1 Sam. 12:22.

22   For v.23b, cf. v.9b; for v.24a (kwn po., c_d-c_{wlm}), cf. v.13b.

23   Apart from this, Dtr.'s work is in evidence in vv.1b,7a ("judges of Israel"), 11a[a] (supplementing br'šwnh in v.10), 11a[b].

24   Alt 1936: 149ff.

25   Weiser (1939: 129 [ET 1961: 163f.]) takes the same view of the original arrangement in 2 Sam. 5 as has been presented above. It is inconsistent of him to support Alt's thesis when he does not agree with its premises.

26   It is scarcely possible to maintain that the report of the victory over the Philistines, which consolidated the position of

David's dual kingdom against erosion from outside, was incomplete in the context of the history of David's rise because it failed to mention David's political measures against the Philistines which could have been recorded in 8:1b.

27   Cf. below pp.58f.

28   An error in the text introduces the formulaic conclusion as early as v.6b; v.12 was added later.

29   2:11 is probably a later addition but knowledge of it is assumed in 1 Chron. 29:27. It was composed on the analogy of 1 Kings 11:42 where Dtr., exceptionally, gives the duration of the reign at the end of a king's reign, because Solomon came to the throne before the end of David's reign and so this information could not be accommodated at the beginning. (The same is true of the information given for the duration of Jeroboam I's reign, in 1 Kings 14:20a.) In the later addition 2:11, the traditional seven and a half years of David's residence in Hebron is rounded off to give seven years. The figure seven and a half was not a later calculation, because, in conflict with the apparently rapid succession of events in 2 Sam. 5, it has David stay in Hebron long after the death of Eshbaal (2 Sam. 2:11; 5:5; cf. 2 Sam. 2:10a). Then the total of 40 years for David's reign could also be based on the old tradition even if the repetition of this figure in the account of Solomon (1 Kings 11:42) makes it look suspiciously like one of Dtr.'s fabrications; similarly the round number 30, given for David's age at accession in 2 Sam. 5:4 looks as though it was invented rather than derived from a traditional source (cf. also 2 Sam. 2:10a).

30   Rost (1926: 89ff.) is certainly right to assign the verses 1,*2,5-9 to the old pre-Deuteronomistic material.

31   Rost 1926: 89.

32   Cf. the chronological summaries in 6:37-38; 7:1. The information from the annals was compiled according to subject matter by Dtr.'s source before him; Dtr. would certainly have put the temple and all that pertained to it (ch. 6 and 7:13ff.) in a single section.

33   For evidence that 8:1ff. and 9:25 originally belonged together see below, n.45.

34   A later writer meant to do away with the censure in 3:3b by adding 3:20. There only the people (not the king) make sacrifices at the "high places" and this is justified by the circumstances. 3:3b is intended as mild censure, not just an objective description of the situation before the completion of the temple, as is shown by the introductory rq. 3:1 was added

later, being woven out of 9:24.

35   This story was obviously based on a local tradition attached to the shrine at Gibeon.

36   Dtr. uses this technical term everywhere.

37   Dtr. wrongly applied this list to the whole area of the dual kingdom of Solomon as is shown by the phrase "all Israel" in the heading (cf. 4:1). The catalogue must have been found, in list form, in an official document, as is shown by the fact that the beginnings of lines in the first half, which include the names, are missing (vv.8b,9,10,11,13); the top right hand corner of the page must have been damaged. We cannot determine to what extent the later additions, vv.13b^{a,c},19b^a,19b^b, were the work of Dtr.

38   The original account can be found in 5:2,3,7; to this were added first 5:6,8, then 5:4,5 and last of all 4:20 and 5:1 which are certainly by Dtr. The variants given by the Septuagint for this section (cf. BH^3, ad loc.) can hardly help with literary criticism of the passage as the Septuagint took considerable liberties with the transmitted text throughout the account of Solomon. (See also below Chapter 9, n.31.)

39   5:15ff. is composed throughout with reference to nothing but the building of the temple, which is the only thing of any importance to Dtr.

40   All the same, it is worth noting that only in Dtr. is King Hiram connected with Solomon's buildings.

41   Hiram's words to David in v.21b^b are connected with the story in 3:4-15 (in particular 3:8). For v.26a, cf. 3:12.

42   6:19b was added by Dtr. who saw the temple primarily as the repository of the "ark of the covenant of Yahweh". 6:11-13 is an interpolation; it keeps to the style of Dtr. but was probably not added until after his time.

43   Probably the source also reported the bronze works made for the rest of Solomon's buildings; these Dtr. passed over. No specific reference is made to the temple until vv. 40b, 45, in the summary in 7:40b-45 which was added later.

44   In the original account 7:46 was obviously the end of the section on the bronze works. The passage vv.48-50 stands apart because it contains no detailed information from the sections of the "book of the history of Solomon" on which Dtr. drew.

45   The reference in 9:25a to Solomon's regular sacrifices in the temple seems out of place, but we see from 9:25b, "and so he (Solomon) furnished the house", that this was formerly preceded by an account of the consecration of the temple. If we

also take note of 9:24 then we see that the "book of the history of Solomon" at this point was obviously concerned with the use made of the new buildings. Furthermore, it is striking that sentences in this section repeatedly begin with 'z: 9:24a (instead of the inappropriate 'k we should read with LXX 'z); 9:24b (in the arrangement of this sentence, the "book of the history of Solomon" probably follows the order in the annals of the kings); 8:1; 8:12 (which makes the transfer of the ark and the consecration of the temple happen at different times). Montgomery (1934: 49) is certainly right to regard 'z used in this way as a substitute for a more exact date given in the annals.

46   Verses 7 and 8 were evidently added, but prior to Dtr., in the "book of the history of Solomon" (cf. the ^{c}d hywm hzh in v.8).

47   This technical term is the one normally used by Dtr.; later it was also added secondarily to v.6; here LXX^B still presupposes the original h'rwn.

48   This view comes from the Deuteronomic law; cf. Deut. 10:1ff.

49   8:1a^b,4a,*6 ("in the most holy place"), 10,11 are post-Deuteronomistic additions in the spirit and style of the priestly writing.

50   8:27 and 8:34b were added later.

51   Cf. above p.57.

52   This passage is regarded as post-Deuteronomistic merely because the date of the "Deuteronomistic redaction" is erroneously put too early.

53   Here too reference is made to the reinterpretation of Nathan's prophecy; for v.5 cf. 2:4, 8:25.

54   In vv.15b,17a^{b}b-19 there is an addition, inserted in an unsuitable place; it is a summary, initially fragmentary, of Solomon's buildings in cities other than Jerusalem, together with a concluding sentence which recapitulates the sum total of the king's buildings (v.19b); subsequently v.16, attached to the word Gezer and v.17a^a, an editorial parenthesis, were appended to this addition. Verses 15b,17a^{b}b-19 may also be from the "book of the history of Solomon".

55   On this, cf. above pp.57,61 and n.45.

56   Verses 23-25 (which allude to 3:4-15) appears to have been added later.

57   Verse 27, which disrupts the train of thought, was added later.

58   Verses 10 and 14 were apparently added by Dtr. as

parentheses to the old aetiological story. The chronology in 9:10 means that the part of Solomon's story beginning in 9:1-9 is limited to the last few years of the king's life (cf. 6:38 and 7:1).

59   It is possible that this arrangement, which is meant to be chronological, comes from Dtr.'s source.

60   On this prophetic story see further below, pp.68f.

61   11:29a[a] was added by Dtr. to provide a transition.

62   The word "always" in v.36b[a] shows that this sentence was composed before Dtr., while the Judaean monarchy still existed.

63   Contrary to Dtr.'s usage in the Solomon story, the name "Israel" refers here to the state of Israel.

64   By "a single tribe" Dtr. thinks of Judah (cf. 11:13, also v.32b); but the prophetic story, which had its origin and was composed in the state of Israel, had in mind the tribe of Benjamin (cf. 12:21,23), which was the only one of those tribes which were, strictly speaking, "Israelite" to remain loyal to the dynasty of David; for the apparent arithmetical error in vv.30,31,36ab[a] makes sense only if the prophetic legend tacitly ignored the tribe of Judah, because it thought that its allegiance to the dynasty of David went without saying.

65   In v.33 the verbs were originally in the singular (with reference to Solomon). The last three words of v.35 are an addition.

66   Verse 39b was added with the rest of the Jeroboam story in mind; the same may be true of the entire passage vv.38b[b]-39 (cf. BH[3], ad loc.).

67   The only unusual feature is the reference to the duration of the reign in the final paragraph; on the cause of this irregularity, cf. above, n.29.

Notes to Chapter Nine
THE PERIOD OF THE KINGS OF ISRAEL AND JUDAH

1   Cf. above p.57.

2   It is clear that the Mesopotamian chronological lists with which we are familiar (cf. Gressmann 1926: 331ff., 359ff.) are also later compilations and draw upon official material covering an extended period.

3   Begrich's study of chronology has led him to assume that the earlier history of the "Books of the Chronicles" used by Dtr.

was fairly complicated (1929: 173ff.). Examination of his conclusions must be postponed to a later occasion.

4   In each instance he explicitly refers those who are interested in the "acts" of individual kings to the "Books of the Chronicles".

5   His attitude is exactly the same as that expressed by Dtr. in 1 Sam. 12:14-15,20ff. in his general survey of the monarchical period, namely that the rise of the monarchy was fundamentally due to the perverse will of the people but, once the monarchy was there, it should be given a chance to prove itself.

6   For further detail, see below pp.80f.

7   The nature of the "Deuteronomistic framework" in 1 and 2 Kings with its chronological data and its verdict on the kings is too well known to warrant detailed examination here.

8   There is no excerpt from the "Books of the Chronicles" on Jehu's usurpation, because this is covered in detail by means of a story concerning a prophet which Dtr. has given in extenso.

9   However, he does not mention that the capital was moved to Tirzah.

10   In the wording of v.26b Dtr. has altered a sterotyped expression which recurs in the stories of the prophets he has narrated hitherto (1 Kings 14:10; 21:21; 2 Kings 9:8) but the meaning of which we can no longer determine conclusively.

11   In the second relative clause in v.28, a later writer - probably later than Dtr. - has interpreted the information in v.25 in his own way and, evidently, completely unhistorically.

12   The account usually given of this campaign on the basis of 1 Kings 14 is incorrect in that the real subject of this section is misunderstood. For further detail see Noth 1938b: 278ff.

13   This section does not deal specifically with the temple, but with cultic matters, which were, in any case, important to Dtr.

14   This section comes from the Judaean and not the Israelite "Books of the Chronicles", as is shown by its position within the account of King Asa and by the fact that Asa is usually mentioned only by name whereas Baasha is usually given his full title. Dtr. has inferred from 1 Kings 15:16-22 that there was a lengthy war between Israel and Judah in the decades after the death of Solomon; in keeping with this view, he has incorporated remarks resembling those found in 15:16 into his conclusions to the stories of the first two Judaean kings (14:30; 15:7b); 15:6 and 15:32 were probably not added until later.

15   Here too its position within the account of the Judaean king Amaziah, and the mention of the Judaean king by name alone and the Israelite king by title as well - cf. in particular vv.8,11,13 (emended text) and see n.14 above - indicates that the story comes from the Judaean "Books of the Chronicles", even though the event was none too glorious from the point of view of the Judaeans.

16   'z at the beginning of v.5 as well as "at that time" at the beginning of v.6 obviously replace a precise date (see above, Chapter 8, n.45).

17   The reference in 18:7b, which looks forward to 18:13-16, comes too soon and, in its present position, is meant to cover the whole period of Hezekiah's reign. It cannot be attributed to an authentic source nor can the note, of totally unclear provenance, on a great victory over the Philistines by Hezekiah in 18:8. Dtr. has merely inferred the content of 18:7b from 18:13-16.

18   In v.29 the general historical situation is described incorrectly. Here Dtr. seems to have misunderstood the text of the information in the "Books of the Chronicles" (cf. on this 2 Chr. 35:20) and, in addition, expressed himself badly in his attempt to clarify the brief statement from his source. Cf. Hjelt 1925: 145.

19   The statement that Edom maintained its independence of Judah "to this day" (v.22) means that the victories in 14:7 and 14:22 were only partial. This expression looks back over a long period and cannot possibly come from the annals but could have appeared, at the earliest, in the "Books of the Chronicles" which brought all this information together.

20   Cf. above p.66.

21   The references could certainly have appeared in the official annals. However, since the author of the "Chronicles of the Kings of Israel" undoubtedly ended with a remark on the destruction of the Israelite state, vv.3-4 which, apart from mentioning the embassy to the pharaoh, tell us virtually nothing specific, could come from this source. In that case Dtr. would have replaced the concluding remark in the "Books of the Chronicles" with the sentence taken from 18:9-11. On the other hand, 17:24,29-31 could also have come from the "Books of the Chronicles".

22   In v.2 the initial yhwh should be deleted.

23   On this cf. below p.74.

24   A similar opinion can be given of 1 Kings 15:23b; cf. also

a similar instance in 1 Kings 22:39, discussed above p.65.

25   See further below, pp.70ff.

26   We completely miss the point of the section if we delete v.15b and so remove the rest from the Ahijah story. The arrangement is such that the apparently incomprehensible blindness of Rehoboam makes sense only as a mysterious act of God which confirms the prophecy made by Ahijah in v.15b. Thus the section is shown to be a necessary part of the Ahijah story. On the other hand 12:21-24, in which another "man of God" appears, looks like a later accretion to the Ahijah story.

27   The similarity of 12:31 and 13:3 shows that the intervening passage was added to the Ahijah story later; on its incorporation, see below p.70.

28   The chronological information they provide leads us to impossible or, at least, implausible conclusions about the actual history of King Ahab; but we cannot assume with Morgenstern (1940: 385-96) that a whole story has been lost following vv.1-2a, or that there were any secondary alterations at all, unless the chronological information in vv.1,2a could be attributed to an authentic tradition. Such an attribution cannot be made and the parallel passage 2 Chron. 18:1f. gives no indication that the beginning of 1 Kings 22, as the author of 2 Chron. 18 knew it, was any different from that transmitted to us.

29   We cannot regard all the passages in 1 Kings 20 in which "prophet(s)" appear as later additions to what was originally just a war report (O. Eissfeldt maintains this [in Kautzsch 1922-23: ad loc.], following others). The scenes with prophets appear too regularly for this to be possible, and the supposed war report is clearly arranged to accommodate these scenes. On the question of the original relation of all these stories about prophets to the historical situation, cf. now Jepsen 1942: 155ff.

30   Cf. above p.62.

31   Later 12:2-3a and the name Jeroboam in v.12 were added and the original introduction in v.20 (roughly: "Then they sent for Jeroboam") altered - all this with 11:40 in mind. Verse 20 (at the end of which, incidentally, "Benjamin" was originally named and not "Judah" - cf. above Chapter 8, n.64) was altered by Dtr., or at all events, before the additions in vv.2f.,12 were brought in, since v.20 does not presuppose the presence of vv.2f.,12. The substantial additional material in the Septuagint after 12:24 does not come from an old tradition about Jeroboam which is missing from the Massoretic text; like the similar material added by the Septuagint after 2:46, this was compiled

out of elements in the Massoretic material. Throughout the first half of 1 Kings the Septuagint has taken considerable liberties with the arrangement of the text. The verdict on Jeroboam added by the Septuagint after 12:24 resembles in spirit that in 2 Chron. 13:6f.

32   This prophetic narrative is introduced in 12:32-33. wy^{cl} ^{cl}-hmzbh occurs three times, which indicates that the text was expanded later; it is evident that only the third of the sentences beginning with these words is authentic (v.33b^b). The first of the passages introduced in this way (v.32a^{b}b) misinterprets v.32a^a as if it referred not to a single action but to a permanent institution (the plural in "calves" and "high places" shows that both "so he did in Bethel" and "in Bethel" which follows were added later still). Because of the story which comes next v.33ab^a has to assume once again that a single action was intended.

33   13:2b^b was expressed as it is, and 13:32b was added, with the account of Josiah in mind (cf. 2 Kings 23:20). Likewise Dtr. was thinking of his words in 13:2b^b when he wrote 2 Kings 23:16.

34   In this transition (13:33-34) Dtr. took the sentences 12:31 and 12:30a from the Ahijah story and himself added to them and sharpened them.

35   Verses 14-16 were added by Dtr.; they follow vv.10,11 post festum, put the threat made to Jeroboam in the larger context of the history of the monarchy (v.14) and anticipate the end of the Israelite state (v.15), regarding "the sin of Jeroboam" as the beginning of the end (v.16). Verses 14-16 stand out so clearly as additions to the story that the rest of the Ahijah story can be seen to be pre-Deuteronomistic (cf. what is said about 12:19). Similarly, 12:31 (cf. on the other hand, 13:33b) is not necessarily Deuteronomistic and in any case is not written in normal Deuteronomistic language.

36   Except that 14:20a could not be fitted in earlier.

37   Verses 4,5b^b and 6 are additions. Verse 5a (we should delete the name David) must originally have come immediately after v.3.

38   Verse 15 looks like an addition by Dtr. who, thinking of 15:18, wanted it made known that the treasure of the temple was replenished after 14:25-28.

39   The badly expressed 16:7 was added later; it goes on from v.2b to blame Baasha for exterminating the house of Jeroboam.

40   Dtr. has interpreted the note in the "Books of the

Chronicles" about Ahab's marriage with Jezebel (v.31b^a) to mean that Ahab turned completely away from God and expresses this briefly in vv.31b^b-33a in part with 2 Kings 10:21-27 in mind; further, on the basis of the Elijah stories, he thinks that Ahab generally represents a severe intensification of evil (vv.31a,33b; cf. 21:25,26).

41   The name "Horeb" in 19:8 was obviously added, probably by Dtr. (cf. above p.27).

42   Here too the Septuagint has arbitrarily rearranged the chapter which Dtr. deliberately organised as he did; it puts the Elijah stories back immediately next to each other (chapters 17-19 + 21). 20:43a^b serves as a transition to chapter 21 (cf. 21:4).

43   Verse 20 was added later: it interrupts the speech by God which continues in v.21 and does not finish until v.24, where it gives way to the general reflection contained in vv.25-26. Similarly, v.23 disturbs the sense and is added with 2 Kings 9:36 in mind. The alternation between addressing Ahab and referring to him in the third person in vv.21ff. can be explained by the fact that vv.21b and 24 are established idioms.

44   In keeping with 14:10-11 (16:3-4) the connection with a threat aimed at Ahab personally has prompted Dtr. to refer here somewhat inappropriately, to the "house of Ahab" rather than the "house of Omri".

45   Verse 38 which takes up 21:19 is by Dtr. If it were earlier, we would have to assume that the narratives in 1 Kings 20 and 22 were already connected with the Elijah stories before Dtr.

46   Dtr., thinking of 1 Kings 22:5ff.; 2 Kings 3:11f., regarded Jehoshaphat as praiseworthy - hence his verdict in 2 Kings 22:43 and, probably, the remark in v.47, connected with 15:12a, which is most probably by Dtr. Verse 45 is based on 1 Kings 22 and 2 Kings 3. On vv.48-50, cf. above p.67.

47   Dtr. took 2 Kings 1:1 from 3:5 and put it in what seemed an appropriate place. Quite rightly, he put the formulaic conclusion to the story of Ahaziah (1:17a^b-18) immediately after the Elijah story. A later writer inserted v.17a^{c}b with its chronological reference, which is strangely inconsistent with that in 3:1 and was probably calculated by him on the basis of the textual variants of 1 Kings 22:52 (cf. BH^3, ad loc.).

48   The arrangement here overlooks the fact that the account in 8:1-6 already assumes Elisha to be dead.

49   In 3:6 the name Jehoram was obviously added later.

Similarly 3:11-12 originally mentioned not Jehoshaphat but "the king of Judah" - this is demonstrated in particular by v.12b - and the name Jehoshaphat in vv.7,14 is also a later addition.

50   Dtr. took the note in v.18a[b] from v.26b. Dtr.'s reflection in v.19 is motivated by the historical fact that the Judaean state continued to exist and has reference to a sentence in the Ahijah story (1 Kings 11:36b).

51   9:29 is evidently interpolated. The attempt it makes to synchronise is based on a comparison of 8:25 with 3:1 and ignores the antedating used in these passages.

52   Here too (v.36) as in 1 Kings 11:42 and 14:20a the duration of the reign is given at the end because there was no room for a formulaic introduction.

53   The name Joash in v.14 was added by Dtr.; vv.16,18 have "the king of Israel", which was the original form on its own.

54   Verse 13a[b] was added later; it is not in the style of Dtr.

55   In v.7 Dtr. seems to have used a piece of information from the "Books of the Chronicles" from which he may also have concluded that Hazael was a contemporary of Jehoahaz, as he states explicitly in v.22. However Dtr. concluded from 8:12 that the liberation from the Arameans did not come until after the death of Hazael - he also says this explicitly in 13:24-25. This is how he came to set the story of Elisha's death in the reign of Joash.

56   It is purely by an oversight that the formulaic conclusion to the account of Joash (13:12-13) is repeated in vv.15-16. Dtr. composed v.6 as an explanatory note based on Deut. 24:16.

57   In v.12 Dtr. refers back to his own statement in 10:30.

58   Begrich (1929: 170ff.) is of course right to think that 15:37, unlike 16:5ff., is not an excerpt from the "Books of the Chronicles". We shall not decide, at this point, whether Dtr., who composed 15:37, here attempted to reconcile different chronological systems, as Begrich believes, or whether he merely accepted at face value or misunderstood some entry or other in the "Books of the Chronicles" in the light of 16:5ff.

59   For this reason, Dtr.'s disapproval of Ahaz in 16:3-4 is particularly emphatic.

60   Verses 21-23, which are not connected with what goes before, were added later. The idea that the basic fault of the Israelite state was the break from the dynasty of David is not found elsewhere in Dtr. Therefore, it is not possible to link vv.21-23 directly with v.6 and thereby regard vv.7-20, which are written completely in the spirit of Dtr., as a subsequent

accretion (so, following others, Eissfeldt in Kautzsch, 4th edition).

61   Here the diverse information given in 17:24, 29-31 and in 17:25-28 is pertinently brought together. Verses 33-34a are repeated in v.41; this shows that vv.34b-40 were added later to give further emphasis to the condemnation in vv.32-34a of the inhabitants of the territory of the former Israelite state.

62   On this Dtr. gives us only the brief reference in 18:4b which comes from the "Books of the Chronicles". Instead of further details we have the general statement 18:4a.

63   Because of its connection with 18:13-16 Dtr. has probably altered the traditional order. Verse 20:6a certainly suggests that 20:1-11 formerly preceded 18:17ff. Or was Dtr. in fact the first to combine two series of Isaiah legends (cf. the double account in 18:17-19:37)?

64   The section on Amon (21:19-25) contains nothing of particular interest.

65   In Dtr.'s work, the expression (which is never explained fully) "the book of the law", used in the report of the discovery of the law, 22:8ff. - similarly "the law of Moses" in 23:25 - must refer to the Deuteronomic law; and this is also historically correct.

66   In places the passage shows signs of Deuteronomistic style and language; these could be the result of editing by Dtr., but more probably result from Dtr.'s dependence on the language of the Deuteronomic law and of the period of Josiah. Dtr. could have met with the record as a separate piece unrelated to the "Books of the Chronicles".

67   23:21-25 is not the end of the report of the discovery of the law but was added by Dtr. This is shown by the reference in v.22 to the conception of the period of the "judges" first developed by Dtr.; then by the generalised nature of the statements in v.24; and lastly by the "Deuteronomistic" verdict in v.25.

68   To this introduction Dtr. added, apart from his usual verdict (v.19), the reflection in v.20a and the generalising sentence v.20b which is needed to prepare the way for what follows.

69   These sections are so deeply embedded in Jer. 39-41, that they must be original there. We need only ask whether Dtr. got the Baruch story directly, or through the "Books of the Chronicles of the Kings of Judah" which might have transcribed it for lack of further official material in order to supply the

desired ending to the compilation. Furthermore, comparison of 2 Kings 25 with the parallel passages in Jer. 39-41 concerns only matters of textual criticism which need not be discussed here but can be usefully clarified if we consider Jer. 52; for this chapter in turn is taken from 2 Kings 25 (except for a few additions of its own).

70   Dtr. could have known the date in v.8 because in his time the day of the destruction of the temple was observed as a day of mourning with fasting and the like - this continued in later times (cf. Zech. 7:3,5).

71   It may seem strange that Dtr. does not so much as mention Jeremiah here, after borrowing the whole narrative of the end of the history of Judah from Baruch's account of Jeremiah which is essentially about the personal fate of Jeremiah. But in this context Dtr. was concerned only with public officials.

Notes to Chapter Ten
THE NATURE OF THE COMPOSITION

1   Cf. the convincing discussions in von Rad 1938 [ET 1966].

2   The explanation hinges upon the Book of Joshua. Those who assume that the Pentateuchal sources extend into Joshua lose sight of the connection Dtr. has made between Deut. and Judges and thus of the unity of Dtr. Of course the old Pentateuchal sources must have dealt with the settlement of Palestine by the twelve Israelite tribes, since this was the goal of the "settlement tradition" narrated by their redactors. However, this does not justify us in attributing at any price all of the pre-Deuteronomistic material in the book of Joshua to those Pentateuchal sources. We are merely required to take this material into account somehow (see Chapter 24 [of Über-lieferungsgeschichtliche Studien]). We must stress that the first question which we can legitimately ask about the old material in Joshua amounts to no more than this: if we analyse it carefully from the point of view of literary criticism, can we prove beyond a doubt that we have here continuations of or conclusions to the old Pentateuchal narrative strands? Our analysis must not be influenced a priori by the knowledge that these strands must have culminated in the settlement of the land west of the Jordan. I may say that my exegesis of Joshua

(Noth 1938a) sufficed to answer the above question in the negative, even before I had arrived at the view of Dtr.'s work which I present here.

3   For further detail, see Noth 1943a: Chapter 15.

Notes to Chapter Eleven
THE HISTORICAL PRESUPPOSITIONS

1   Recently the notion that there were two phases of "Deuteronomistic redaction" of the books Joshua-Kings has become popular. But the assumption that the material was first edited in Deuteronomistic style before the exile is based on a mistaken attribution, to this first editor, of all sorts of traditional materials, which in fact come from Dtr.'s sources.

2   Recently, the view that Josiah's law is the same as the basic text of Dt. has been criticised in various ways but it seems to me so well-founded that I can assume it here, without going into the supporting arguments.

3   It seems that the "Book of the Covenant" was unknown in Josiah's time as well as to Dtr. - similarly the "Holiness Code", if it was already in being at that time. The various prescriptions on cult which already existed were not comprehensive laws of the nature of the Deuteronomic law. Nor was the decalogue in the same category as the Deuteronomic law. According to both the secondary introductions of the Deuteronomic law (cf. Deut. 5:1ff., esp. vv.28ff.) and Dtr., the decalogue contained the fundamental words of God on Sinai, and these words received their authentic interpretation through "the law" (= the Deuteronomic law).

4   Cf. Noth 1940b: in particular pp.27ff. [ET 1966: 41ff.].

5   It is hard to tell how far Josiah was constitutionally justified in interfering with the local shrines throughout the land. It was appropriate enough for him to annul the measures taken by his predecessors (cf. 2 Kings 23:5), the basis of which was also of dubious validity. In removing the local shrines he certainly treated the land of Judaea (v.8) in the same way as the conquered land (vv.15,19). Did he think that the law justified him in interfering with the old religious institutions and traditions in such a novel manner? On the possibility that the constitutional basis of the monarchy of the house of David was changed as a result of the events of 701, cf. Alt 1929: 87f.

6   Cf. Noth 1940b: 16ff. [ET 1966: 18ff.].
7   Before Josiah, the last time that we hear of "the law"
being known is in 2 Kings 14:6; perhaps Dtr. assumed that it
disappeared for some unknown reason during the reign of
Manasseh.
8   One crucial omission from his history is the institution of
the sacral alliance between the twelve tribes; he certainly has
no recollection of it and shows no knowledge of its existence in
his account of the periods of the "judges" and the kings, even
though it was probably still in force then (cf. Noth 1940b: 22ff.
[ET 1966:28ff.]).

Notes to Chapter Twelve
ATTITUDE TOWARDS THE MATERIALS IN THE TRADITIONS

1   This is particularly conspicuous in some of the accounts
of cultic activities. See further below, pp.95f.
2   He ascribed indisputable documentary value to the
content of his sources, and he regarded the events reported in
them as historical reality which had to be respected as such.
One can certainly not expect him to take a critical view of the
sources transmitted to him.
3   In this context, it is particularly significant that he says
nothing of Josiah's far-reaching attempt to restore the empire
of David which all kinds of casual references in the tradition
indicate; even though Josiah is one of the few figures in the
Israelite and Judaean monarchical period whom Dtr. counts as
outstanding and worthy of unqualified praise. He has made a
point, therefore, of passing over the king's political and military
achievements - any casual reference to them certainly has a
very specific reason. He does the same in his treatment of
Omri, Ahab and Jeroboam II, and it is quite wrong to explain
this, as many do, on the grounds that he disapproved of these
kings.
4   But the introductory topographical information in Deut.
1:1b-2 comes from a source otherwise unknown to us (see above
p.27).
5   Cf. above pp.48ff.
6   Dtr. probably found Ramah named as the home of
Samuel in other sources as well (cf. above, Chapter 7, n.38); but
the specific reference to the altar to Yahweh built by Samuel

there (1 Sam. 7:17) looks very much like a particular local tradition attached to the place.

7   This includes the report on the appearance of Samuel's sons in Beersheba (8:2) which can be attributed to the re- markable religious connections between Beersheba and the shrines of southern Samaria. Cf. Zimmerli 1932.

8   Perhaps we should include the short passage added in 2 Kings 23:4b[b].

9   It is tempting to conclude that this is where Dtr. himself lived and wrote - it is perfectly possible.

10   The "Books of the Chronicles" did not categorically refrain from mentioning prophecies (1 Kings 16:12; 2 Kings 14:25). We can understand that they gave no report of the pro- phetic writers' threats, since as little official attention as possible would have been paid to these in the kings' court.

11   In this context it is pertinent to mention Dtr.'s simplified version of the itinerary of the Israelite tribes' wanderings in the wilderness in Deut. 2:1ff. (cf. above pp.29f.). Similarly Dtr.'s general summaries of separate historical periods are intended to explain and structure the work as a whole in the interests of clarity and lucidity.

12   We need not enquire here whether Mount Ebal was originally mentioned at this point; cf. the commentaries.

13   Even though Dtr. has incorporated material from a separate account of Samuel and Saul into 1 Sam. 7:2-8:22 and 10:17-27a (see above p.50), his main concern in these chapters is not to report these separate items but to interpret the action in general along what he considers the right lines.

14   Only 1 Kings 5:15-32 could be adduced as a formal counterpart.

Notes to Chapter Thirteen
THE CENTRAL THEOLOGICAL IDEAS

1   On this traditional material, cf. von Rad 1938 [ET 1966].

2   Following his source (cf. 'z in 1 Kings 8:12, and on this see Chapter 8, n.45) Dtr. has regarded the moving of the ark and the dedication of the temple as two separate actions performed at different times, both related to sacrificial practices.

3   Subsequently the temple retained its significance as the

place towards which prayers were directed, cf. Dan. 6:11 and the fact that the synagogues of which we know in the period after Christ faced Jerusalem.

4   Of course the story in Dan. 6 (cf. n.3 above) has been transposed into the exilic period when the temple had been destroyed and sacrificial worship temporarily suspended.

5   Naturally this also applies to Manoah's sacrifice in Judg.13:19f. but, like the rest of the story of Samson, this story was probably not added to Dtr.'s account until later.

6   Elijah's sacrifice took place when the Jerusalem temple was standing - Dtr. considered this the sole lawful centre of cult and his view covered the Israelite kingdom as well, as is shown by his running commentary on the Israelite kings. Here then Dtr. makes extraordinarily large concessions to the tradition, even if this is an exceptional case. Furthermore, the appearance of this particular instance in the Books of Kings, which are agreed to be the work of a "Deuteronomistic editor", i.e. compiled by a Deuteronomistic writer, shows that the occurrence of similar sacrificial scenes in 1 and 2 Samuel does not prove that they do not belong to Dtr's work.

7   Cf. von Rad 1929: 60ff.

8   Cf. von Rad 1929: 70f.

9   It is striking that such additions are found only in Deut. and not in Joshua-Kings, where there was every opportunity to supplement the text in a similar way. We must conclude that this revision was not carried out until Deut. had been detached from the body of Dtr.'s work and included in the Pentateuch; (cf. on this, Chapter 25 [of Überlieferungsgeschichtliche Studien]). Given its role as a canonical document for the post-exilic community, the Pentateuch could not tolerate the idea that the destruction of Jerusalem in 587 was the final end. Meanwhile this revision did not affect the rest of Dtr.

10   The fact that Dtr. had access to such a variety of literary sources might suggest that he had stayed behind in the homeland rather than being deported. The preservation of these sources must at the very least indicate that they survived the great catastrophes; they would be most readily available in the homeland. Besides, the best explanation of Dtr.'s familiarity with local traditions attached to the region of Bethel and Mizpah (cf. above p.85) would be that he lived in Palestine and, better still, this particular region. Finally, it would seem more likely that one of those who stayed in the land would omit to express any expectation for the future.

BIBLIOGRAPHY

Albright, W.F.
1935   "The Names Shaddai and Abram", Journal of Biblical Literature 54, pp.173-204
Alt, A.
1929   "Die territorialgeschichtliche Bedeutung von Sanheribs Eingriff in Palästina", Palästinajahrbuch 25, pp.80-88 (= Kleine Schriften zur Geschichte des Volkes Israel, vol. 2 [1954], pp.242-49)
Alt, A.
1931   "Judas Nachbarn zur Zeit Nehemias", Palästinajahrbuch 27, pp.66-74 (= Kleine Schriften zur Geschichte des Volkes Israel, vol.2 [1954], pp.338-45)
Alt, A.
1934   Die Ursprünge des israelitischen Rechts, Berichteüber die Verhandlungen der sächsischen Akademie der Wissenschaften zu Leipzig, philologisch-historische Klasse, 86 (= Kleine Schriften zur Geschichte des Volkes Israel, vol.1 [1953], pp.278-332) (ET "The Origins of Israelite Law", in Essays on Old Testament History and Religion [1966], pp.79-132)
Alt, A.
1936   "Zu II Sam 8₁", Zeitschrift für die alttestamentliche Wissenschaft N.F. 13, pp.149-52
Begrich, J.
1929   Die Chronologie der Könige von Israel und Juda
BH³
1937   Biblia Hebraica, ed. R. Kittel
Bleek, Fr.
1878   Einleitung in das Alte Testament, 4th edition
Budde, K.
1890   Die Bücher Richter und Samuel, ihre Quellen und ihr Aufbau
Budde, K.
1897   Das Buch der Richter (Kurzer Hand-Commentar zum Alten Testament, VII)
Chapman, W.J.
1935   "Zum Ursprung der chronologischen Angabe I Reg 6₁", Zeitschrift für die alttestamentliche Wissenschaft N.F. 12, pp.185-89

143

Driver, S.R.
1913   Notes on the Hebrew Text and the Topography of the Books of Samuel

Eissfeldt, O.
1925   Die Quellen des Richterbuches

Eissfeldt, O.
1931   Die Komposition der Samuelisbücher

Eissfeldt, O.
1934   Einleitung in das Alte Testament (ET of 3rd edition: The Old Testament. An Introduction [1965])

Grether, O.
1939   "Die Bezeichnung 'Richter' für die charismatischen Helden der vorstaatlichen Zeit", Zeitschrift für die alttestamentliche Wissenschaft N.F. 10, pp.110-121

Gressman, H.
1926   Altorientalische Texte zum Alten Testament, 2nd edition

Hempel, J.
1930   Die althebräische Literatur (Handbuch der Literaturwissenschaft)

Hjelt, A.
1925   "Die Chronik Nabopolassars und der syrische Feldzug Nechos", Beihefte zur Zeitschrift für die alttestamentliche Wissenschaft, 41 (K. Marti Festschrift), pp.142-47

Hölscher, G.
1922   "Komposition und Ursprung des Deuteronomiums", Zeitschrift für die alttestamentliche Wissenschaft 40, pp.161-225

Jepsen, A.
1942   "Israel und Damaskus", Archiv für Orientforschung 14, pp.153-72

Kautzsch, E.
1922-3 Die Heilige Schrift des Alten Testaments, 4th edition

Kuenen, A.
1890   Historisch-kritische Einleitung in die Bücher des alten Testaments, I, 2

Koning, J. de
1940   Studien over de El-Amarnabrieven en het Oude-Testament

Möhlenbrink, K.
1938   "Die Landnahmesagen des Buches Josua", Zeitschrift für die alttestamentliche Wissenschaft N.F. 15, pp.

Bibliography

238-68

Montgomery, J.A.

1934 "Archival Data in the Book of Kings", <u>Journal of Biblical Literature</u> 53, pp.46-52

Morgenstern, J.

1940 "Chronological Data of the Dynasty of Omri", <u>Journal of Biblical Literature</u> 59, pp.385-96

Musil, A.

1907 <u>Arabia Petraea</u> I

Noth, M.

1935 "Studien zu der historisch-geographischen Dokumenten des Josua-Buches", <u>Zeitschrift des Deutschen Palästina-Vereins</u> 58, pp.185-255 (= <u>Aufsätze zur biblischen Landes- und Altertumskunde</u>, vol.1 [1971], pp.229-80)

Noth, M.

1938a <u>Das Buch Josua</u>

Noth, M.

1938b "Die Wege der Pharaonheere in Palästina und Syrien. IV. Die Schoschenkliste", <u>Zeitschrift des Deutschen Palästina-Vereins</u>, 61, pp.227-304 (= <u>Aufsätze zur biblischen Landes- und Altertumskunde</u>, vol.2 [1971], pp.73-93)

Noth, M

1940a "Der Wallfahrtsweg zum Sinai (4. Mose 33)", <u>Palästinajahrbuch</u> 36, pp.5-28 (= <u>Aufsätze zur biblischen Landes- und Altertumskunde</u>, vol.1 [1971], pp.55-74)

Noth, M.

1940b <u>Die Gesetze im Pentateuch</u> (Schriften der Königsberger Gelehrten Gesellschaft, Geisteswissenschaftliche Kl. XVII, 2) (ET "The Laws in the Pentateuch: Their Assumptions and Meaning", in <u>The Laws in the Pentateuch and other studies</u> [1966])

Noth, M.

1940c "Num. 21 als Glied der 'Hexateuch'-Erzählung", <u>Zeitschrift für die alttestamentliche Wissenschaft N.F. 17</u> (1940/41), pp.161-89

Noth, M.

1941 "Beiträge zur Geschichte des Ostjordanlandes. I. Das Land Gilead als Siedlungsgebiet israelitischer Sippen", <u>Palästinajahrbuch 37</u>, pp.50-101 (= <u>Aufsätze zur biblischen Landes- und Altertumskunde</u>, vol.1 [1971], pp.347-90)

145

Nowack, W.
1902   Die Bücher Samuelis
Rad, G. von
1929   Das Gottesvolk im Deuteronomium (Beiträge zur
Wissenschaft vom Alten und Neuen Testament, III, 11)
Rad, G. von
1938   Das formgeschichtliche Problem des Hexateuchs
(Beiträge zur Wissenschaft von Alten und Neuen
Testament, IV, 26) (ET "The Form-Critical Problem
of the Hexateuch", in The Problem of the Hexateuch
and other essays [1966], pp.1-78)
Rost, L.
1926   Die Überlieferung von der Thronnachfolge Davids
(Beiträge zur Wissenschaft vom Alten und Neuen
Testament, III, 6)
Rudolph, W.
1938   Der 'Elohist' von Exodus bis Josua (Beihefte zur
Zeitschrift für die alttestamentliche Wissenschaft, 68)
Sellin, E.
1933   Einleitung in das Alte Testament, 6th edition [ET of
3rd edition: Introduction to the Old Testament (1923)]
Staerk, W.
1894   Das Deuteronomium
Steuernagel, C.
1923   Das Deuteronomium, 2nd edition
Weiser, A.
1939   Einleitung in das Alte Testament (ET of 4th edition:
Introduction to the Old Testament [1961])
Wellhausen, J.
1895   Prolegomena zur Geschichte Israels, 4th edition (ET
of 2nd edition: Prolegomena to the History of Ancient
Israel [1885, r.p. 1957])
Wellhausen, J.
1899   Die Composition des Hexateuchs und der histor-
ischen Bücher des Alten Testaments, 3rd edition
Wiese, K.
1926   Zur Literarkritik des Buches der Richter (Beiträge
zur Wissenschaft vom Alten und Neuen Testament,
III, 4)
Zimmerli, W.
1932   Geschichte und Tradition von Beerseba im Alten
Testament

INDEX OF BIBLICAL REFERENCES

JOURNAL FOR THE STUDY OF THE OLD TESTAMENT
Supplement Series